Two Egg, Florida

A Collection of Ghost Stories, Legends and Unusual Facts

Dale Cox

2007

ISBN: 9781441409751

Second Printing

4514 Oak Grove Road
Bascom, Florida 32423

www.twoeggfla.com
www.exploresouthernhistory.com
www.battleofmarianna.com

Contents

Introduction

When you grow up in a community named Two Egg, you learn to have a sense of humor about your place in life. And, I suppose, about life in general.

The truth be told, I grew up in the "suburbs." Parramore is a small community nestled in the gum swamps and pine woods. Two Egg, just a few miles away, was the nearest place we could buy a Coke or candy bar or anything else we needed or wanted. We always stopped at one of the stores there on our way for a swim at Blue Springs after a day of picking vegetables in the hundred degree heat of summer.

Even today, going back home is like stepping through time. Two Egg is still there, but the stores have closed. I enjoy the sight just the same. When you leave the paved highway and drive down the dusty roads, it is like living the old life again. Cell phones don't work once you get too far into the pines. High speed internet is available I suppose, but most people don't have a need for it. Instead, they still walk in the evenings, fish with cane poles, talk about snakes and alligators, comment on Sunday's sermon and wonder how the watermelons will do this year.

For me, it is always a good reminder of what the world once was and probably should be again. No matter what you are told, you can still go home. And the trip is usually worth the journey.

I began writing this on a visit home. I've lived all around the country and been asked thousands of times about the unique place where I grew up. Just hearing the words "Two Egg" always seems to bring smiles to the faces of inquisitive friends. So I sat down to write the story of my home as best I know it. The result, as you will see, is a collection of stories from Northwest Florida, all of them true to one degree or another. Each has fascinated me at some point in my life and I hope that as you read them, you will find yourself intrigued as well.

Dale Cox

Figure 1: Two Egg, Florida

Figure 2: Downtown Two Egg

Chapter One

The History of Two Egg

Long before anyone ever thought of naming this crossroads after that most famous of breakfast delicacies, the place that would become Two Egg was at least a spot on a trail.

Archaeological discoveries in the area tell us that this was once an important hunting and manufacturing center for Native Americans. Artifacts recovered from the fields around Two Egg date back thousands of years to the archaic period, a time when prehistoric hunters roamed the vast woods in search of deer, turkey and other animals, especially buffalo. A chert or flint outcrop not far from today's crossroads has been identified as a quarry, where these people came to chip away rocks to use in fashioning tools such as points, knives, scrapers and drills. They didn't necessarily live here for long periods of time. The shortage of surface water was a problem for them. They came steadily, though, seeking game and raw materials, establishing a pattern they would continue for thousands of years.

By around the time of Christ, significant civilizations were developing both to the east and west. Large villages grew along the margins of the ponds and swamps just a few miles east of Two Egg, the inhabitants of which built mounds for the burial of their dead. A few of these mounds still survive, but most have been either looted or unintentionally destroyed by farming or timber operations. When the Spanish arrived in Florida during the 1500s, the Two Egg area was uninhabited but situated almost equidistant between three powerful and important Native American chiefdoms.

The first of these, the Chacato or Chatot, claimed ancestral rights over all of what is now eastern Jackson County. Sometimes incorrectly confused with the Choctaw, the Chacato lived in key villages just west of the Chipola River. They considered the land between the Chipola and the Chattahoochee/Apalachicola as their primary hunting ground and were more than willing to use military force if necessary to protect their territory.

Early Spanish writers, in fact, noted that neither the Apalachicoli who lived up the Chattahoochee River nor the Apalachee who lived around what is now Tallahassee had much interest in challenging the Chacatos. When a peace treaty was arranged between the three groups in 1639, the governor in St. Augustine remarked that it was "an extraordinary thing" because the Chacatos "never had peace with anybody."

Despite their independence, some of the Chacatos eventually agreed to allow Franciscan missionaries to enter their villages. It was not a unanimous decision and half the nation revolted the next year, 1675, destroying the missions and forcing the missionaries to flee for their lives. Fray Rodrigo de la Barreda, who served at the mission of San Carlos west of the Chipola, was wounded with a blow to the head by a stone axe but survived. He described fleeing on foot without either food or shoes and making his way through the woods along a secondary route to the mission of Santa Cruz de Sabacola in the forks of the Chattahoochee and Flint Rivers (today's Lake Seminole). Since the main trail from San Carlos to Sabacola passed across the Natural Bridge of the Chipola and by Blue Springs on its way to the mission, Barreda's route undoubtedly was farther north. It is possible that he took the old trail passing across the site of Two Egg.

The Chacato uprising was crushed by the Spanish, who sent a military force into the region. The conflict so weakened the Chacato that they were unable to defend themselves against subsequent raids by the Creeks and English and their presence in Florida was all but wiped out. By 1706, all of the Chacato were gone and for the first time in thousands of years, no one hunted in the woods of Two Egg.

For more than a decade, no humans at all lived within many miles of today's Two Egg crossroads, but by around 1716 a few bands of Creeks began to make their way down the Chattahoochee to resettle old fields and hunt in the vast woods. The process accelerated after 1763 when Spain surrendered Florida to England at the end of the French and Indian War. Larger groups of Creeks started coming down the Chattahoochee, laying the foundation of what would become the Seminole Nation of Florida.

The Creeks by this point had become dependent on European supplies and luxuries, so traders followed them into the region to establish trading posts where Native American hunters could trade their deerskins for guns, ammunition and other goods. One of these trading posts, operated by a half-Spanish, half-Creek individual called "the Bully," stood at the town of Ekanachatte or "Red Ground" on the Chattahoochee River. The site of this village is recognizable today as Neal's Landing. A similar trading post was established by a half-English, half-Creek trader named Thomas Perryman on the east bank of the Chattahoochee due east of Two Egg. Both traders enjoyed commanding monopolies because their fathers had married into the royal lines of their villages.

The establishment of these villages and stores led to the creation of a crossroads at Two Egg. Since Ekanachatte was located where the primary trail from Pensacola to St. Augustine crossed the Chattahoochee River, it became a well-known and important village and crossing place. The inhabitants, after receiving the gifts their culture taught them to expect, would assist travelers across the river. To reach Ekanachatte from Pensacola, it was necessary to follow the old Pensacola-St. Augustine Road east along roughly the same route as today's State Highway 2. The path included several difficult crossings over tributaries of the Chipola River at Forks of the Creek. When water was low, travelers usually made faster time by swinging south and crossing the Natural Bridge at today's Florida

2

Chapter One

Caverns State Park. From there, the "low water" trail led back northeast and rejoined the main road at Ekanachatte. This trail passed just a few miles west of Two Egg.

A second route, meanwhile, developed from the Natural Bridge to Perryman's Town. This trail followed the routes of today's State High 69 and Green Road, passing directly across the site where Two Egg now exists.

A convenient cut-off trail soon developed to connect this second road with the "low water" trail to Ekanachatte. This cut-off joined the Perryman Trail at Two Egg, forming the crossroads that can still be seen today. Although the roads are wider and better maintained today, their configuration has not changed much in 230 years.

By the time of the American Revolution both English and Native American travelers routinely used these paths, crossing the present site of Two Egg on their way to and from Ekanachatte and Perryman's Town. Florida reverted to Spanish control at the end of the Revolutionary War, but both roads remained in use.

After the First Seminole War of 1817-1818, settlers drifted down into the upper reaches of today's Jackson County. Even though Florida was still Spanish territory, a significant community developed along Spring Creek just north of Campbellton. The nearest frontier outpost where these settlers could obtain supplies was Fort Scott, a military post about ten miles up the Flint River from its confluence with the Chattahoochee in today's Decatur County, Georgia. To open communication with the fort, they chopped a trail down from Spring Creek to the point on the Chipola where Bellamy Bridge stands today. From there the trail extended to connect with the old Perryman Trail near Greenwood. After 1820, when Isaac Fort established a plantation at the future Bellamy Bridge site, the path became known as the Fort Road in his honor. It still bears that name today.

Over the next two decades, traffic increased considerably over the future site of Two Egg. Riverboats arrived on the Chattahoochee River and a series of landings developed. Cotton plantations grew along both the Chipola and Chattahoochee and by 1840 virtually all of Jackson County's best lands, at least by the standards of those days, had been claimed. Over the next two decades, farming spread into virtually all of the remaining agricultural land and by 1860, on the eve of the Civil War, Jackson County had grown into one of Florida's three largest counties with a population of over 10,000.

It was during this period that the future site of Two Egg was settled for the first time. Property records indicate that Joseph T. Michaux filed for ownership of the site of Two Egg on July 1, 1857. Alfred S. Knowles filed for the adjoining lands to the east on the same day. This does not provide a firm date for settlement of the community. Property ownership usually reflected that the sites had already been occupied for some time.

Very little is known of Michaux. His name does not appear on the 1850 census for Jackson County and by 1860 he seems to have either no longer been alive or no longer living there. Three children, ages 6, 8 and 10 bearing the

Two Egg, Florida

Michaux name do appear on the 1860 census as residents of the home of Harriett and Benjamin Bazzell. It is unknown if Harriett was their mother, but the Bazzell family is closely associated with the history of the Lovedale – Two Egg area. It is logical to assume that the children were the prodigy of the community's first settler.

Alfred Knowles, meanwhile, is a somewhat better known individual. He married Martha Heath of Jackson County on October 31, 1858, a little over one year after staking his claim to the half-section of land at Two Egg. According to the 1860 census, he was living a few miles northwest of Marianna and working as an overseer. Why Alfred was not living on the land he owned at Two Egg is not clear, but perhaps he needed the money from his job to support his little family that had grown to include a 10 month old girl named Alice.

Whatever the plans of the family, they were put on hold by the War Between the States. Knowles enlisted in Company E, 2nd Florida Infantry Battalion (Confederate) on August 8, 1862 at Merritt's Bridge near Marianna. He fought at the Battle of Olustee and was still with his battalion when it was consolidated with other companies to form the 10th and 11th Florida Infantry Regiments in June of 1864. Sent to Virginia, Knowles fought as a member of Finegan's Brigade in Robert E. Lee's Army of Northern Virginia. Like tens of thousands of other soldiers, however, he became severely ill and was hospitalized at Howard's Grove, Virginia, on October 5, 1864. A few days later he was given furlough to return home. His destination was officially listed as Port Jackson, a riverboat landing on the Chattahoochee connected by direct road with Marianna.

Like many others of his era, Alfred Knowles never recovered. He died shortly after reaching home. Just five years earlier he had been the promising 25-year-old head of a growing young family. Now he was just another victim of the deadliest war in American history. He left a desperate wife and three young children, Alice, James and Jenny. As was common then, Mrs. Knowles remarried quickly to a Confederate veteran named Samuel Basford on December 20, 1866. The 1870 census found them living near Paront, a small community south of Dellwood, with a growing brood of five children.

Although these first settlers did not prosper in their efforts to establish homes at Two Egg, others followed with better success. Slowly a community began to grow at the crossroads. The emergence of an important naval stores center and river port at Parramore during the 1890s helped, as the growing little community that would become Two Egg lay on the primary road connecting Parramore with Greenwood and Marianna. A road leading south from Bascom to Dellwood and the railroad at Grand Ridge also helped, making sure that commerce bound for the trains passed through almost daily. An Alabama company responded by extending a railroad south from Cottonwood to Malone and Greenwood, providing another shipping point for the farmers, timber and naval store interests of Northeastern Jackson County.

Chapter One

By the early 20th century, a business community began to grow. First there was a general store and then another. The Allison company built a sawmill there and the community soon came to be called Allison in honor of the family's contributions to its growth. The name might have lasted, but instead disaster came once again. When Michaux and Knowles first tried to settle the crossroads, the Civil War destroyed their efforts. Now, when Allison was showing signs of growth, the harshness of the Great Depression swept across the South.

As the economic disaster grew, money dried up and jobs disappeared. Families struggled to survive and, as local cemeteries attest, hunger, malnutrition and sickness stalked the land. By 1930 many local families were living on little more than pride. Unable to pay for items they needed in hard cash, they began to barter and trade with the storekeepers in Allison for the things they could not do without. The merchants could then sell the farm products they obtained this way in larger communities, keeping their own families fed and their businesses alive.

In the darkest days of the Great Depression, many families in Jackson County literally survived day to day. The harder things got, the less they had to trade, especially during the off season when crops and gardens weren't coming in. In fact, about all they could depend on were a few eggs a day to get them through to the next. And at certain times of the year, eggs were virtually all they had to trade for anything else they might need.

The origin of the name Two Egg can be traced to these hard times. There are dozens of stories that explain how the name came about, most of them similar in one way or another. Outsiders often seem fascinated with the fact that there are so many stories, but for locals it is just a fact of life. A South Florida newspaper once claimed that citizens were prone to fistfight over which version was right, but this was a preposterous claim. If anything, there was always a mild curiosity although everyone generally agreed on the key points.

The story told by John Henry Pittman, who for many years ran the store originally established by the Allison family, is fairly simple. Two young boys came into the store so often on an errand from their mother to trade two eggs for sugar that regulars jokingly began calling the establishment a "two egg store." The name, according to Mr. Pittman, caught on and was picked up by traveling salesmen and others who spread it to nearby towns.

Most of the other stories are similar. Some replace sugar with candy and others say the story originated after the storekeeper lost his temper and yelled something to the effect of, "Two eggs, two eggs! This is just a two egg town!" Other versions credit traveling salesmen or "drummers" with originating the name. These men, who usually sold items such as patent medicine, were common fixtures on the back roads in their day.

Whichever version you accept, the story may seem light-hearted on the surface, but at a deeper level it reflects an effort to put a good face on very hard times. During the darkest years of the Depression, many families in the area were surviving on little more than biscuits and cornbread. Spring and summer brought corn, peas and beans, but these ran out long before spring brought more. Although it is difficult to conceive in this day of "low carb" diets, carbohydrates are a vital necessity of life. Carbohydrates provide the body with energy and help key organs function properly. Without them, the body quickly descends into the listless state easily recognized in people who are under-nourished. They occur naturally in whole grains, fruits and vegetables, but in the hardest seasons of the year, these were hard to obtain. The key alternative to these, of course, is sugar. A little sugar added to the diet each day provided just enough energy to help struggling families make it through to the next day. In other words, two eggs worth of sugar could make the difference between life and death among people already living on the edge of collapse. It puts a different face on the significance of that legendary trade of two eggs for sugar.

The implementation of the New Deal and the creation of work programs through the Works Progress Administration and Civilian Conservation Corps brought jobs back and with them the salaries needed to start the economy on the road to recovery. People soon began to use money instead of eggs at Two Egg, but the name stuck. It appeared on the official highway map of the State of Florida in 1940 and has remained there ever since.

Many stories are told by veterans and their families of landings at distant air fields during World War II where they saw signs pointing the way and number of miles back to Two Egg. My father, Clinton Cox, who served for twenty years in the U.S. Navy, has told many times of being summoned at the urgent request of his commanding officer. Wondering what trouble he might be facing, he arrived only to be presented a copy of *Life* magazine. Two Egg was on the cover.

The *Life* article began a national fascination with Two Egg. It has since been featured in *National Geographic* Magazine, in hundreds of other articles, on television programs, in short stories and on the internet. When the stores were still open, they sold Two Egg t-shirts, car tags, towels and beach balls. One even offered fake diplomas from "Two Egg Tech" University.

There is, of course, much humor and fun in all of this. Local residents generally take it with a wink and a smile, but their accomplishments should not be lost in the humor that attends the name of their community. Members of the Green, Tyus, Pittman, Hewett, Cox and other families have served Jackson County in a variety of elected posts. Academy Award winning actress Faye Dunaway lists nearby Bascom as her official birthplace, but her family is spread throughout the Two Egg area. In 1990 she told *Fame* magazine that she came from a poor farming family and is a living example of the American Dream. Members of the Long family worked with grace and distinction to help end racial segregation in the local school system. The community has produced business people, soldiers, sailors, educators, public servants, journalists, farmers and others who have achieved in a wide variety of areas. James W. Hart, Jr. retired from the U.S. Air Force Reserve as a Brigadier General. He is listed in *Who's Who in America*.

Chapter One

Finally, there was Susie Hartsfield. A groundbreaker in many ways, Mrs. Hartsfield was born into slavery and lived a long and amazing life. When she was more than 100 years old, she achieved widespread acclaim by enrolling at Chipola College in Marianna. The news coverage generated by her accomplishments shattered notions of what seniors could achieve and inspired others to follow in her footsteps.

The stores in Two Egg are closed today, but travelers still stop to pose and smile by the highway signs at the edge of town. Jackson County is experiencing an economic upsurge and undoubtedly in time the community will rebound, just as it has many times before. Until then, though, Two Egg is a wonderful reminder of what it always has been and hopefully will continue to be, a peaceful place where life is still lived as it was intended.

Figure 3: Bellamy Bridge

Figure 4: The Ghost? Notice the mist in the lower right corner of the photograph.

Chapter Two

The Ghost of Bellamy Bridge

A few miles north of Marianna, the Chipola River flows silently beneath the rusting framework of an old iron bridge. Historic in its own right, Bellamy Bridge is one of the last surviving such structures in Jackson County. It takes its name from previous spans that crossed the river at this point, but it is undoubtedly best known as the centerpiece of a fascinating Florida legend.

The Bellamy Bridge ghost story is Jackson County's most enduring legend. Several residents of the county, all in their eighties and nineties, indicated in 1986 that they were told the story by their parents, who had heard it from their own fathers and mothers. This would date the origin of the legend to at least the late 19th century. The story also first began to appear in print at about the same time, indicating that it was common knowledge by the beginning of the 20th century. This is a reasonable timetable, since the legend revolves around a young woman named Elizabeth Jane Bellamy, who died in 1837. Her overgrown and often-vandalized grave is a few hundred yards south of Bellamy Bridge in the edge of the river swamp.

As the story goes, Elizabeth was the young bride of Dr. Samuel C. Bellamy, a prominent member of early Florida society. This fact is verified by her headstone, as is the date of her death, May 11, 1837. The rest of the story, however, has been handed down by word of mouth through the years and sometimes repeated in local newspapers. Although there are numerous variations, the most common revolves around the courtship and wedding of Elizabeth and Samuel. Enamored of his young bride, who had promised to love him forever, Samuel built a large columned mansion for her in Marianna. The wedding date was set for May 11, 1837, and was to be the biggest event of the social season in the growing plantation community. Guests, it is said, began to arrive a full week before the wedding and gifts came from as far away as Europe. Samuel and Elizabeth, according to the story-tellers at least, were wed in the rose garden behind the magnificent home, but their happiness was short-lived. There are two stories of what happened next. The first holds that while dancing a waltz during the elaborate reception, they moved too close to a burning candle. The other claims that exhausted from the rigors of the day, Elizabeth sank into a comfortable chair to rest. Her dress somehow came into contact with a lit candle. As to what happened next, both stories are the same. The young bride's elegant gown burst into flames and before the groom or any of their guests could react, she ran from the house in panic and was engulfed by fire. She lingered for days but ultimately

9

succumbed to her injuries and was buried beneath a grove of trees on the plantation of Samuel's older brother, Edward.

The grave, however, could not contain the love and devotion that had grown between Samuel and Elizabeth. The young groom went nearly mad with grief, turned to the bottle and ultimately committed suicide. He refused to ever live in the beautiful mansion he had constructed for his bride, and for many years the finest home in Marianna remained dark and vacant. Elizabeth, local residents say, was unwilling to leave her true love behind. An apparition began to appear on dark and foggy nights, wandering the swamps around the small cemetery where she was buried. It was said to be that of Elizabeth, the young bride, who ventured from the grave each night in search of her husband. Some have described her as a pale image in a long, white gown, moving slowly along the riverbank. Others say that she is engulfed in flames, screaming as she makes a mad dash for the nearby bridge and river. The third story holds that the ghost can be seen plunging from mid-air straight down into the waters of the Chipola.

It is a fascinating tale and a unique reminder of the time when story-telling was a leading form of entertainment among residents in Northwest Florida. The story is certainly old. Many of the key parts of the legend have come to be accepted as true, particularly the wedding-night death of Elizabeth Bellamy and the grief-stricken descent into lunacy of her husband. Much of the story, of course, is shrouded in legend. The Bellamy Bridge tale is unique in Florida folklore, however, because it deals with identifiable people and actual dates. Both Samuel and Elizabeth Bellamy were prominent members of early Florida society and as such, their story is actually quite easy to trace.

Dr. Samuel C. Bellamy was born in North Carolina in 1810 and graduated from the medical school of the University of Pennsylvania in 1834. Not long after, he and his brother, Edward, moved south to Florida. They were associated with a group of prosperous North Carolina residents who sought to develop the rich lands along the upper Chipola River and were closely allied with the individuals who had founded Marianna in 1827. Exactly when they arrived is not clear, but real estate records indicate it was probably in late 1835 or early 1836. They developed extensive holdings in land and quickly became two of the largest planters in the county. Both owned dozens of slaves. Edward focused primarily on farming, but Samuel was interested in business and politics.

The two brothers were also closely connected with the Croom family. Major General William Croom of Lenoir County, North Carolina, was one of that state's largest property-owners and the father of numerous children, including two daughters named Ann and Elizabeth. When he died in 1829, he left the girls extensive real estate holdings as well as slaves and other wealth. The Croom family was by then already strongly interested in the new territory of Florida. One of the general's sons, Hardy Bryan Croom, became a noted planter and naturalist in Florida and his home, "Goodwood," is now preserved as a Tallahassee area museum. Edward and Samuel Bellamy were closely associated with the men of the Croom family and it is logical that they soon developed romantic connections with the daughters of the general.

After a standard courtship of the time, Ann married Dr. Edward C. Bellamy in 1829, the same year as her father's death. According to newspaper records in North Carolina, the couple was married at the family home in Lenoir County. Elizabeth, who was called "Eliza" in her father's will, was then only 10 years old.

The exact point at which she became romantically involved with Samuel C. Bellamy is not known. The two families had lived near each other in North Carolina and the two may have been close friends for many years. Certainly following the courtship and marriage of Ann and Edward, the bond between the two families tightened. As Elizabeth reached her mid-teens, she was courted by Samuel, who was her senior by nine years. Since Samuel went away to medical school in Pennsylvania, much of this courtship was probably carried out by correspondence.

From this point, however, the true history of the marriage departs significantly from the legend. Family correspondence indicates that Samuel and Elizabeth were married in North Carolina on July 15, 1834, three years before the date of the supposed Florida wedding. The true wedding date, however, is confirmed by North Carolina newspapers of the time, which note that the ceremony took place in Newington, Lenoir County, North Carolina, the community were Elizabeth was born and raised. She was 15 years old when she took Samuel Bellamy's hand in marriage.

Like Edward and Ann, the couple moved to Jackson County, Florida. Although legend holds that Samuel constructed the large mansion in Marianna for his new bride, surviving documentation indicates otherwise. The records of the Union Bank of Florida, of which Samuel became an appraiser, indicate that he was awarded 148 bank shares worth $14,800 on February 10, 1838, for use in building a new home. Since Bellamy was identified as a resident of Marianna at the Florida Constitutional Convention in St. Joseph later that year, this loan was undoubtedly the source of funding for the construction of the mansion. Based upon the currency of the day, $14,800 would have allowed him to build a substantial residence and the magnificent home was in fact a showplace for many years. Located in the center of a full city block bounded by Green, Clinton, Market and Jefferson Streets, the Bellamy mansion was the largest home in the city of Marianna. It would have been a grand wedding gift, but Elizabeth never saw the home as the loan for its construction was approved nine months after her death.

The couple, instead, undoubtedly lived on Samuel's Rock Cave Plantation near Marianna. The estate included hundreds of acres of cultivated land and was farmed by the forced labors of more than 80 African slaves. King Cotton was then booming and planting was an extremely profitable venture in Florida, especially for individuals with the means to put together large gangs of slave laborers to clear the fields and cultivate the cotton. The little family grew. Samuel and

Two Egg, Florida

Elizabeth had a baby boy in late 1835, giving him the name Alexander after several of Samuel's ancestors. It was, probably, the happiest time of their lives.

The happiness, unfortunately, was not to last. The bottomlands of the Chipola River were indeed ideal for the production of cotton, but they were also breeding grounds for vast swarms of mosquitoes. Deadly fevers, including malaria, ravaged the growing population throughout the early history of Jackson County. The young Bellamy family was not spared. According to a December 6, 1836, letter from Hardy Bryan Croom, Elizabeth's half-brother, to his wife, the fevers had hit particularly hard that fall. Samuel, Elizabeth and baby Alexander were all suffering from what likely was malaria. The deadly fever was often described by doctors of the time as the "intermittent and remittent" fever because patients often improved, only to relapse and in many cases die. Samuel C. Bellamy, in fact, did recover from the fever, but his wife and child did not. According to an obituary in the Tallahassee *Floridian*, eighteen-year-old Elizabeth Jane Croom Bellamy, as her tombstone records, died on May 11, 1837. She was not the victim of a tragic wedding night fire, but died instead of a mosquito-borne fever. Her eighteen-month-old son Alexander, according to the same obituary, died seven days later on May 18, 1837.

Elizabeth and the baby were laid to rest in the small family cemetery near the banks of the Chipola River near the present bridge site. Certainly Elizabeth's sister, Ann, cared for the graves. The correspondence of Hardy Bryan Croom, who soon died in a tragic shipwreck, includes letters of condolence to Samuel as well as expressions of gratitude from the grieving husband for the sympathies extended him by members of his wife's family. The legend is correct in its supposition that the loss of Elizabeth was a blow from which Samuel Bellamy never recovered. He never married again and fell into spells of dark depression and alcoholism. A letter written by Samuel to the Crooms indicates that he hoped to take Elizabeth's body back home to North Carolina and bury her in a cemetery around which he planned to construct a rock wall. Why he changed his mind is not known.

Despite the legend to the contrary, the loss of his wife and child did not end Bellamy's useful life. After a time of mourning, he turned his attention to business and politics. Appointed an appraiser for the Union Bank, an early "planter's bank" with offices in Tallahassee and Marianna, Samuel became involved in the bank's practice of reappraising property as values increased, giving land owners expanded lines of credit and larger mortgages. It was risky business and a practice that ultimately brought down the bank when Florida's economy weakened and land values fell. It was during this period of obvious prosperity, however, that Samuel borrowed money for and constructed his mansion in Marianna.

In keeping with his status as one of the leading residents of the new community, he was selected as one of four delegates from Jackson County to the Florida Constitutional Convention of 1838. Meeting in the coastal boomtown of St. Joseph (on the site of today's Port St. Joe), the delegates hoped to forge a constitution by which the territory could be become a state of the expanding

Union. As the meeting began, Bellamy delivered an important speech to the assembled delegates:

> *...Many of us...are not politicians by profession; we do not look to politics as an object from whence to derive support for our families, we take no delight in party strife or political turmoil – but have come here with another view, and are influenced by no other motives, than to discharge honestly the trust committed to us by our constituents, and to lay the foundation of the government, which we humbly hope is to advance the future prosperity and happiness of the good people of Florida.*

The convention was a success. Bellamy served on the banking committee and was an active participant in the drafting of Florida's original constitution.

Returning to his mansion in Marianna, he continued his duties as an appraiser for the Union Bank. Although he never remarried, legend that he never lived in the house is untrue. Unfortunately, any hopes he might have entertained of quickly rebuilding his personal life were soon shattered. In 1840, cotton prices began to fall as a failure of the national economy rippled over into Florida. Property in the state was overvalued and when cash flow dwindled, many planters found themselves unable to pay their bank notes. Devastating hurricanes lashed the Gulf Coast and a Yellow Fever outbreak in 1841 virtually depopulated the city of St. Joseph. Nearly 12,000 residents had once flooded the coastal city, terminus of the first railroad in Florida, but after the fever just a couple of hundred remained. Many of the houses were dismantled and relocated to nearby Apalachicola, but the ones that remained were destroyed in a terrible hurricane and tidal surge in 1844. Florida's largest city simply disappeared from the face of the earth.

The effect of such devastation on the emerging territory was overwhelming. By 1841, as the crisis deepened, the Union Bank was faced with default. An investigation by Congress the following year found that the bank had engaged in extravagance and that its mortgage practices far exceeded its resources. As the situation worsened, the bank collapsed and by 1843 had closed its doors for good. Samuel Bellamy by this time owed $27,710 to the bank and was faced with legal action when he found himself unable to pay his loans. The remains of the unfortunate man's life collapsed. That he was seeking any and all means of improving his financial state is evidenced by the 1844 contract awarded him by Jackson County for the construction of a wooden bridge across the Chipola River at the site of today's Bellamy Bridge.

Samuel attempted to sooth his woes with alcohol, but descended into severe alcoholism. It was at this time that his brother Edward gained control over Rock Cave Plantation. Whether this was originally done as a way of protecting the property from Samuel's creditors or whether Edward took the action because of his brother's descending mental state, the move led to great friction between the two men. In 1848, Samuel ran an ad in the Florida *Whig* offering his services as a physician, noting that he had no other means of supporting himself because of the wrongdoing committed against him by his brother. On July 4, 1849, he spoke in telling words of the powers of alcohol during a rally in Marianna. "The cup is offered," he told the crowd, "He seizes it with the avidity a drowning man would catch at a straw, and buries alike his sorrows and his senses in oblivion." That Samuel tried to fight his alcoholism is apparent from his affiliation with the Chipola Division of the Sons of Temperance that same year. That he failed is equally apparent.

Although he served as a Justice of the Peace and Clerk of Courts in Jackson County, he was never able to recover his fortune. The magnificent mansion in Marianna was sold to U.S. Attorney C.C. Yonge and by 1850, Samuel was living with the family of James Baker in Marianna. He and Edward never reconciled. Although the man had clearly descended into depression and alcoholism, he was given a job in 1852 as deputy clerk of the Supreme Court of Florida. How effectively he discharged his duties is subject to question, as by 1853 he clearly was severely depressed and possibly suicidal. In this condition he revised his will, instructing the executor of his estate to "prosecute to the limit of the law against Edward C. Bellamy, until he shall be compelled to account for and pay over the last cent he has had of mine." The court later decided in Samuel's favor, but most of the money recovered was taken to cover the judgment obtained against him by the Union Bank.

On December 28, 1853, sixteen years after the death of his wife and child, Samuel C. Bellamy took his own life. He was 43 years old. According to Charles Hentz, a local resident, he killed himself by slashing his own throat with a razor at the ferry landing in Chattahoochee. Both Hentz and the local press reported that he was "laboring under delirium tremens" and had been "exceedingly intemperate for years past."

The story of the lives of Samuel and Elizabeth Bellamy is tragic almost beyond belief, and it is not difficult to see how a ghost story could have grown from the terrible circumstances. But how such a story could have evolved into the form it takes today is difficult to comprehend. Elizabeth did not die on her wedding night and the cause of her death was fever, not fire. Yet the story is so intensely believed in Jackson County that it has become an accepted part of local history. The answer, surprisingly, may be found in the writings of a 19th century novelist named Caroline Lee Hentz.

One of the most popular writers of her day, Caroline Hentz was a prolific author best known for a noteworthy series of romantic novels. She and her husband Nicholas traveled from town to town across much of the eastern United States, living at times in North Carolina, Ohio, Alabama, Georgia and finally Florida. Mrs. Hentz was best known in her lifetime for her politically-charged novel, *Planter's Northern Bride*. The novel was a rebuttal to Harriett Beecher Stowe's *Uncle Tom's Cabin*. Both women had been members of the same literary guild in Cincinnati and Mrs. Hentz was outraged by Stowe's portrayal of life and slavery in the South. *Planter's Northern Bride* was acclaimed across the cotton states as a more accurate portrayal, but was poorly received in the North. It should be noted that, despite her role as the author of the rebuttal to *Uncle Tom's Cabin*, Hentz was quick to recognize the abilities of individual African Americans. She played a key role in the development and literary training of at least one African American poet and actively attempted to secure his freedom from slavery.

Mrs. Hentz spent the final years of her life in Columbus, Georgia, and Marianna, Florida. In 1853, three years before her death, she published a fascinating little volume titled *Marcus Warland or the Long Moss Spring*. Mrs. Hentz was then a resident of Columbus and she based the novel on the life she lived and observed in the Chattahoochee River valley. The book is unique in that it includes detailed descriptions of daily events in the slave communities on the large plantations of the region. One of the subplots of the book, in fact, tells of the fiery wedding night death of a young woman named Cora:

> *...Turning away she threw herself into a large easy-chair in front of the fire, and in spite of the excited state of her feelings and the extreme want of sentiment evinced by the act, she fell asleep in her downy nest. She had been up almost all the preceding night, on her feet all day, and had been dancing with such extraordinary enthusiasm, that the soft cushion and gentle warmth of the room soothed her to instantaneous repose. How long she slept, she knew not. She was awakened by a sense of heat and suffocation, as if her lungs were turned to fire. Starting up she found herself encircled by a blaze of light that seemed to emanate from her own body. Her light dress was one sheet of flame, the chair she left was enveloped in the same destroying element.*

The story bears a striking resemblance to the Bellamy Bridge legend. The young bride in *Marcus Warland*, however, was not the darling child of antebellum aristocracy. She was Cora, a young slave on a large plantation. Her mistress was so attached to her that she arranged for her wedding to be held in the main house and even provided her with the finest of settings, including an elegant wedding gown. The name chosen by Hentz for the mistress of the plantation, as might be expected by this point, was "Mrs. Bellamy." The story, in fact, reads almost like a recitation of the Bellamy Bridge legend:

> *"Mercy! Mercy!" she shrieked. "Oh! Mistress, save me, save me." Rushing through the hall and down the stairs, the flames flashing more wildly round her, she still screamed, "Mistress, save me!" Mrs. Bellamy, who was in the room below, heard the*

15

sudden terrible cry of human suffering, and flew to relieve it.
When she beheld the blazing figure leaping towards the open
door, and recognized the voice of Cora, shrill and piercing as it
now was, regardless of self, she sprang after her, and seizing
her with frenzied grasp, tried to crush the flames with her
slender fingers, and smother them against her own body. While
she was thus heroically endeavoring to save the beautiful
mulatto at the risk of her own life, Hannibal, who had dragged
the carpet from the hall, wrapped it closely around the form of
her he so madly loved....

Hannibal, was a man Cora had passed over when she selected another of the
Bellamy slaves, King, as her husband. The story goes on to relate how the young
woman was so severely burned that she writhed in misery for days before finally
succumbing to merciful death. Her groom, King, remained by her side the entire
time, in "frantic agony, sobbing and wringing his hands, and calling piteously on
her name." The fire that claimed Cora's life began when she nodded off in a chair
and her dress came into contact with a candle burning on a table. She was buried
in small cemetery on the plantation, her grave surrounded by flowers and shrubs:

...The mourning bridegroom of an hour planted a weeping-
willow by its side, and many a night, when the moon was
shining on her grave, the tall, dark form of Hannibal would
wander to the spot, certain that he met there the spirit of Cora,
and that she looked kindly upon him. Indeed, all the negroes on
the plantation saw her ghost, and it was always dressed like a
bride, in white muslin, white roses, and white kid gloves.

It is, without doubt, the identical story preserved by the legend of Bellamy
Bridge, and it appears to have been true. In the "Address to the Reader" at the
beginning of the book, which she datelined in Columbus, Mrs. Hentz elaborated
on the story of Cora's death:

The description of Mr. Bellamy's plantation is drawn from the
real, not the ideal. The incident recorded of Mrs. Bellamy, of
her endeavouring to rescue the mulatto girl from the flames at
the risk of her own life, occurred during the last winter in our
city. The lady who really performed the heroic and self-serving
deed is a friend of our own, and we saw her when her scarred
and bandaged hands bore witness to her humanity and
sufferings.

Chapter Two

The actual identity of the Columbus resident whose story Mrs. Hentz developed into that of "Mrs. Bellamy" is not known, nor is the actual name of the young bride she desperately tried to save. The rest of the transition of the story from real event to fictional literature to Florida folklore quickly becomes apparent.

Soon after she published *Marcus Warland*, Caroline and Nicholas Hentz relocated to Florida. Her sons Charles and Thaddeus already lived there. She spent her remaining years in the small resort at St. Andrews Bay and finally in Marianna. Ironically, one of the largest homes in the town when she lived there was the very house built by Samuel Bellamy nearly thirty years earlier. Caroline Lee Hentz died in 1856 and was buried in the small cemetery at St. Luke's Episcopal Church.

Marianna in its early days considered itself something of a haven for society and culture and the city quickly adopted Caroline Hentz. For many years after her death, she was regarded as the community's most famous resident. Her books were widely read in Jackson County and, because she had lived her final years in the area, many local residents assumed she had written them there. The description of the "long moss spring" in *Marcus Warland*, for example, was long believed to have been a literary picture of Jackson County's beautiful Blue Spring. In truth, though, Mrs. Hentz had not yet seen the spring when she wrote the book and the description is of a similar pool near Columbus. In much the same way, the story of the unfortunate bride who died in a wedding night fire on the Bellamy Plantation became an accepted part of Jackson County's folklore.

Over time, the memory of Caroline Hentz and her books faded. Few people today have read *Marcus Warland*. But even though the book itself was forgotten, the tragic story it told of a young bride and a horrible wedding night fire was too poignant to forget. Probably due to Hentz's use of the name "Bellamy" in her book, the story came to be associated with the lonely grave of Elizabeth Jane Bellamy at Bellamy Bridge. Over time, Elizabeth became the focal point of a story that now made its transition from literature to folklore.

And so, a small bit of Caroline Hentz lives on in her final hometown. Elizabeth Jane Bellamy did not die on her wedding night, but the story of her wandering spirit preserves the true story of a young woman who did. *Marcus Warland* has evolved into a new form, just as Hentz used real life situations in Columbus, Georgia, to weave her fascinating tale. The two women, "Cora" and Elizabeth, never met in life but have become united in death. Both of their stories live on, although merged under a single identity.

As for the ghost itself, people still claim that a restless apparition roams the swamps around Bellamy Bridge. It must be admitted that the true facts of the story do not disprove the legend. If anything, they add depth to it. If ever true history warranted a ghost, the example can be found in the story of Elizabeth and Samuel Bellamy and the forgotten young bride, "Cora."

Figure 5: Caroline Lee Hentz, Creator of the Bellamy Bridge Legend

Figure 6: The Samuel Bellamy Mansion

Figure 7: Bellamy Bridge

Figure 8: A smiling son of Two-Toed Tom?

Figure 9: A Florida Alligator

Chapter Three

The Legend of Two-Toed Tom

The story was old even before writer and University of Alabama professor Carl Carmer heard it during the 1930s. Deep in the swamps along the Alabama-Florida border, residents told tales of legendary battles with a monster they called "Two-Toed Tom." Carver was fascinated with the story and included it in his critically-acclaimed but controversial book, *Stars Fell on Alabama*.

When Carmer first learned of Two-Toed Tom, at some point during the 1920s, the beast was described as a "red-eyed hell-demon" in alligator form, about fourteen feet long and greatly feared by the rural residents along the Florida line near Florala. The reptile had been well-known in the area for more than twenty years and was accused of eating cows and mules and even blamed for assaulting several local women. According to Carmer, the monster received its name from the unusual footprints it left behind. Supposedly he had lost all but two of the toes on his left front foot to a steel trap. Two-Toed Tom also had survived numerous shootings and at least one dynamite attack, none of which seemed to have bothered him.

The well-known dynamite attack was launched after the alligator emerged from the swamps near Florala and killed a mule on the farm of a local resident named Pap Haines. The farmer had been waging a twenty year war with Two-Toed Tom and was so irate over the loss of his mule that he decided to go after the beast with as much firepower as possible.

According to Carmer's account, Haines and his son packed fifteen syrup buckets with sticks of dynamite, lit the fuses, and threw the buckets into the pond where the alligator was believed to be hiding. The explosions shredded every living thing in the pond, uprooted trees and sent geysers of water high up into the air.

No sooner had they ended their attack, however, than the men – now joined by eight of their neighbors – suddenly heard a monstrous splashing sound from another nearby pond. The splashes were punctuated by the sounds of screams. By the time all the men could reach the scene, all they could see were the red eyes of Two-Toed Tom sinking into the pond. The half-eaten remains of Haines' twelve year old granddaughter were found on the shore.

Carmer ended his account by noting that local residents had heard reports that Tom had crossed the border into Florida. What Carmer could not have known at the time he wrote his book, however, was that the story of Two-Toed Tom was far from over.

Two Egg, Florida

A wave of sightings of a giant beast soon spread through the Choctawhatchee River and Holmes Creek swamps of Holmes, Walton and Washington Counties, Florida. Cattle and livestock disappeared from farms and the countryside was generally terrorized by this new threat that had crossed the line from Alabama.

Suddenly, in the midst of this rash of sightings, several Florida newspapers reported that a logging crew in Walton County had killed an alligator of enormous size. According to an article in the *Holmes County Advertiser*, the reptile was eighteen feet long and more than eight feet across the shoulders. If the measurements are correct, it was the largest alligator killed in Florida during the modern age. The generally-accepted record was a full six inches shorter than the beast described in the *Advertiser* account.

The Walton County alligator, however, was not Two-Toed Tom. Upon examination his left front foot was found to be fully intact. Tom was still on the loose and everyone in the region knew it.

Not long after, a monstrous alligator was spotted in Sand Hammock Lake, a large body of water near Esto in northern Holmes County. The monster could be heard bellowing every morning at the northern end of the lake and, according to Holmes County historian E.W. Carswell, it was not long before people began finding tell-tale two-toed tracks in the sand.

The size of the alligator was said to be tremendous. A group of local teenagers who saw him reported that he was much larger than previously estimated. Estimates ranged from eighteen to twenty-four feet. Efforts to kill him with rifles and shotguns failed.

Perhaps the most terrifying event involving this incarnation of Two-Toed Tom took place when he suddenly walked onto a dirt road near Esto, coming directly between a mother and her four year old daughter. Historian Carswell located the girl from the story in 1989 and this writer accompanied him to interview her.

She was an elderly woman then and told a fascinating story of returning from a family vegetable garden, lagging behind her mother as children often do. The gigantic alligator suddenly walked into the road in front of her. Either hearing or sensing the reptile's presence, her mother turned around and began to scream. The huge alligator responded by raising himself up onto his four feet, a position from which a normal alligator can run at speeds of up to thirty miles per hour. He made a loud hissing noise as he did so.

Neighbors came running from all directions and someone summoned a man named Harmon Holland, ancestor of well-known area outdoorsman and television personality "Red" Holland. Mr. Holland came with his old "war rifle" and shot the alligator to death at close range.

Everyone assumed once again that Two-Toed Tom had been killed, but when the dead reptile was examined he was found to have all of his toes. He also proved to be slightly less than fourteen feet long – and not quite dead. When someone tried to cut off his tail for meat, he suddenly awakened and sent those standing close by flying with a swing of his tail.

Even more concerning was the fact that the large alligator was but one of many fleeing from Sand Hammock Lake. Tracks were discovered all along the south shore indicating that alligators were moving out of the lake. Since male alligators will move into new territory if confronted by a "bull" of overwhelming strength and size, local residents deduced that something huge must have moved into the lake. To have been big enough to drive a fourteen foot long alligator from the lake, it must have been large indeed.

The bellowing and sightings in the lake soon stopped, however, and residents around Esto relaxed, assuming that Two-Toed Tom had moved on to a new location.

Where he went for the next fifty years, no one knew, but the legend continued to be told. In the 1980s, however, people who remembered the tales were stunned by news that Two-Toed Tom apparently was still alive. The region was experiencing a near record drought. In dry weather conditions, alligators and other animals will often alter their habits to find water. At Boynton Island near the confluence of Holmes Creek and the Choctawhatchee River, an alligator "slide" or path of enormous size was discovered. A closer look revealed that a monstrous gator had walked across a sandbar and climbed the muddy bank to the island. Close inspection of the tracks revealed that one of its feet had only two toes.

The news touched off a rash of new sightings. Some eyewitnesses described seeing a "Loch Ness Monster" like creature in the Choctawhatchee River, while others soon reported him back in Sand Hammock Lake. The town of Esto took advantage of the opportunity and local residents launched a Two-Toed Tom Festival in honor of their most famous resident. Stories were featured in local newspapers and on area television stations. NBC Nightly News even ended its broadcast one night with video of determined monster hunters searching for Two-Toed Tom.

As of this writing, no one has found him. The sightings have died down again, but deep bellows are still heard from area swamps. And if the volume of the sounds is any indication, Two-Toed Tom is still out there somewhere, growing bigger with each passing year.

Figure 10: Alum Bluff, Site of the Garden of Eden?

Figure 11: Branch of a Torreya Tree, Florida's Legendary "Gopher Wood"

Chapter Four

The Garden of Eden

If you turn off State Road 20 onto State Road 12 in the small but picturesque Liberty County town of Bristol, just ahead on the left you will see a sign pointing the way to the Garden of Eden. It is located, appropriately enough, on Garden of Eden Road. On this site, some local residents believe, man's history on the earth began.

The Garden of Eden is one of the best known parts of the Book of Genesis. After He created the heavens and the earth, the plants and the animals, God created man. The first man was named Adam and, as a place for him to live, God created a magnificent garden:

> *Now the Lord God had planted a garden in the east, in Eden; and there he put the man he had formed. And the Lord God made all kinds of trees grow out of the ground – trees that were pleasing to the eye and good for food. In the middle of the garden were the tree of life and the tree of the knowledge of good and evil.*
>
> **Genesis**
> **Chapter 2, verses 8-9.**

The Garden of Eden was watered by a river that flowed from four headwaters. One of these came from a land where there was gold, the second wound through the land of "Cush," the third was the Tigris and the fourth was the Euphrates. Because God did not think it was good for Adam to be lonely, He created a woman named Eve to live in the garden as well. Adam was warned, however, that he was not to eat from the tree of the knowledge of good and evil. If he did, he would die.

What happened next is well known. The serpent tempted Eve to eat of the tree of the knowledge of good and evil and she shared the fruit with Adam. God then drove them both from the Garden of Eden and placed cherubim (Angelic beings) before the entrance to the garden and a flaming sword that flashed back and forth to guard the tree of life. These protected the garden until the flood of Noah, when the Garden of Eden was washed away.

It has long been assumed that the Garden of Eden was somewhere in modern day Iraq. The Tigris and Euphrates Rivers still flow there and the region has long been called the "Cradle of Civilization." A more controversial theory, however, holds that the garden was nowhere near the Middle East. This theory, first

25

advanced by Bristol resident E.E. Callaway, places the Garden of Eden on Florida's Apalachicola River.

For Callaway, this theory was not just a flight of fancy. The Apalachicola is fed by four primary tributaries or "heads," exactly like the river described in the Book of Genesis. In addition, some of the rarest plants in the world grow along the bluffs and steephead ravines on the east side of the river between Bristol and Chattahoochee. Among these are both the Florida torreya and the Florida yew. The torreya was officially discovered by botanist Hardy Bryan Croom during the 1820s and named for Dr. John Torrey, a famed naturalist of the time. Locals have long called it the "stinking cedar" for the strong odor it emits when it is bruised. They also believe it is the famed gopher wood from which Noah built the ark. This legend, of course, added strength to Callaway's theory that he had found the Garden of Eden.

Seeing a Florida torreya today, it is difficult to imagine that Noah or anyone else could have built an ark from its wood. The trees are generally small and spindly, but this was not always the case. Photographs exist of massive torreya trees growing in the woods near Chattahoochee. Disease infected the trees during the 20th century, however, and almost the entire population was wiped out. Today, only young specimens survive and state, federal and private preservationists are doing what they can to try to save and bring them back.

Callaway's ideas about the Garden of Eden caught on, particularly in and around Bristol. The story became widely known throughout the area and some true believers went so far as to erect informational signs at Alum Bluff, centerpiece of Callaway's garden, pointing out locations where Adam might have met Eve, where the Tree of Life grew and more. The signs no longer exist today, but photographs of them can be found in the Florida State Archives.

The site identified by E.E. Callaway as the Garden of Eden is protected today as part of The Nature Conservancy's Apalachicola Bluffs and Ravines Preserve. Accessible via Garden of Eden Road, the preserve has paid tribute to the local legend by labeling a primary trail leading through the site as the Garden of Eden Trail. Be aware though, this is not a walk for the faint of heart.

The trail leads from a parking lot and informational kiosk near Highway 12 to the crest of Alum Bluff, a walk of 3.75 miles, much of it up and down. The scenery, however, is spectacular. Clear, bubbling streams flow through the bottoms of the steephead ravines. There are rare plants and animals, some of which are found nowhere else in the world. And at the end of the trail is Alum Bluff, a magnificent elevation that provides what may be the best view in all of Florida. Towering 135 feet above the Apalachicola River, the bluff is believed to be the largest exposed section of the earth's crust in Florida. The trail guide map, available at the kiosk, provides information on the uniqueness of the setting and also points out the site where Callaway believed the Garden of Eden once existed.

Torreya trees do exist in the preserve, but they are not visible from the trail. The best place to actually see them is nearby Torreya State Park. Located just upstream at Rock Bluff, the state park offers a number of amenities not found in the more pristine Apalachicola Bluffs and Ravines Preserve. The view from the bluff at Torreya is not as spectacular as that from Alum Bluff, but it is a lot easier to reach.

On the left side of the brick path leading from a parking area up to the historic Gregory House, a beautiful antebellum home that once stood across the river, a board fence surrounds a planting of torreya trees. An adjacent marker tells the story of the tree, its discovery and near disappearance. Torreya trees can also be seen at other locations in the park.

Torreya State Park also offers camping, picnicking, hiking, guided tours of the Gregory House and the remains of an earthwork artillery battery built by Confederate troops during the Civil War. A similar battery also stood at Alum Bluff, but it has largely been lost to erosion.

Another torreya tree grows next to the sidewalk leading to the visitor's center at Florida Caverns State Park near Marianna. Although this park is outside the known historic range of the tree, the environment there is quite similar to the Apalachicola River bluffs.

Figure 12: Historic Gregory House, Torreya State Park

Figure 13: William Augustus Bowles

Figure 14: Chattahoochee River from the site of Ekanachatte

Chapter Five

Jackson County's Pirate Treasure

In the extreme northeast corner of Jackson County is a remote area of swampy ponds that is home to legends of international intrigue and buried pirate treasure. Most of the stories center around one particular body of water, barely distinguishable from others nearby, except for the tradition of local residents that it is the "Money Pond." They believe that millions of dollars in stolen gold and silver remain hidden beneath the cypress-stained water of the pond, stashed there to prevent its capture by U.S. soldiers during the early 1800s.

The story originates with the late 18th century activities of a nefarious adventurer named William Augustus Bowles. This is the same individual who is celebrated today by the Billy Bowlegs Festival in Fort Walton Beach, although there is no evidence he ever actually used the Bowlegs name. He was probably too fond of hearing his real name to take on an alias.

Born in Maryland before the American Revolution, Bowles joined a Loyalist regiment there and came to Pensacola as a soldier. Military life did not agree with him and he soon walked away from the service, finding shelter among the Lower Creek villages along the Chattahoochee River. Despite his earlier falling out with the British military, he led some warriors from these villages back to Pensacola to assist in defending the city against a Spanish attack during the Revolution. The attack succeeded, however, and the paroled British garrison was sent to New York by the Spanish.

Bowles eventually made his way back to the Chattahoochee country, where he took up residence in the Perryman Town on the east bank of the river in what is now Seminole County, Georgia. Marrying one of Perryman's daughters, Bowles fathered several children before he was 19 years old. He also began to dream of greater things. His father-in-law, Thomas Perryman, was by this time the principal chief of the lower towns, what today would be considered the Seminole Nation.

Bowles conceived a plan to create an empire among the lower towns that could contend with the United States and the European powers that still maintained designs on Native American lands. To assist in this plan, he enlisted the support of Perryman and other chiefs, including "the Bully" of Ekanachatte and Kenhajo of Mikasuki. A Georgia trader, James Burges, also joined his organization.

With such assistance, Bowles declared an independent nation that he called the "State of Muskogee." Adventurers from both the Bahamas and the United States joined him and he soon provoked a "war" with Spanish authorities in Florida. After the Spanish attacked and burned his headquarters, Bowles retaliated by forming what he called the "Navy of Muskogee" and issued orders for his captains to raid Spanish shipping on the Gulf of Mexico.

This navy, in truth, was little more than a small squadron of pirate ships. The real motivation behind Bowles' activities from the beginning was to seize control of the highly profitable Native American fur trade from firm of John Forbes and Company. The establishment of the Muskogee "Navy" gave him a chance to raid the shipping of his competitor, as well as vessels flying the Spanish flag. Despite his brief capture and subsequent escape from Spanish prison, Bowles also forced the surrender of the fort of San Marcos de Apalache at St. Marks and raided the Forbes and Company storehouses on the Wakulla River.

In some of his surviving correspondence, he mentioned plans to bring a small ship bearing plunder up the Apalachicola to either Perryman's Town or Ekanachatte. What became of the ship or the plunder it carried has never been determined. Bowles was captured again in 1804 and this time died in Spanish prison, never to return to his "State of Muskogee."

His partisans, however, remained active along the lower Chattahoochee and legend holds that they secreted their plunder at Ekanachatte, a Lower Creek village on the site of today's Neal's Landing in Jackson County. The village was the home of a powerful chief and trader known as "the Bully" who was described by a contemporary as the wealthiest man in the Creek country. He died at some point prior to the War of 1812 and leadership of the village passed to his nephew, an individual known as Econchatimico or "Red Ground King."

Econchatimico was one of the chiefs who aligned against the United States during the First Seminole War of 1817-1818 and his town was targeted by a large force of U.S. Creek Auxiliaries operating in conjunction with the advancing army of Major General Andrew Jackson. Ekanachatte was attacked and destroyed on the morning of March 13, 1818. More than 150 women and children were taken prisoner and 20 men killed. Econchatimico and the rest of his people, however, escaped by fleeing west toward the Chipola.

According to legend, though, they left behind their greatest treasure. It is said that the chief ordered that Bowles' wealth be thrown into the "Money Pond" to prevent its capture by the U.S. forces. The gold and silver sank deep into the muddy bottom of the pond, where it remains to this day.

There has been at least one major expedition to find the treasure and, surprisingly, some silver was recovered. The treasure hunters went into the swamp and began a long, slow draining of the pond. Once the water was out, they began excavations and almost immediately started to uncover pieces of Spanish silver. Before they could find the main treasure, however, the entire project was driven from the swamps by a sudden rise of the Chattahoochee River. The pond refilled with water and without the financing needed to try again, the expedition came to an end.

The site of Ekanachatte was occupied by settlers from Georgia when Florida was transferred from Spain to the United States. The old fields of the village were farmed again and a new community grew over the ruins of the old. A mill was constructed on Irwin's Mill Creek, the ruins of which remain today and homes and cabins were built throughout the area.

Econchatimico and his people relocated to a new village site downstream near where Butler Road intersects with the River Road north of Sneads. They remained there until 1838 when they were removed by troops under future President Zachary Taylor and forced to relocate to new homes in what is now Oklahoma. Many of the chief's followers became statistics on the "Trail of Tears."

At their former home site near Irwin's Mill Creek, a log raft was built to carry people back and forth across the Chattahoochee River. Many of Jackson County's earliest pioneers reached their new lands by crossing on this barge. When steamboat traffic arrived on the river, a riverboat landing was established adjacent to the ferry. According to legend, the site was given the name Neal's Landing when a newspaper reporter called across the river from Georgia to ask the name of the new settlement. Members of the Neel family, who established the landing, answered back. The name was misspelled in newspaper articles and continues to be spelled "Neal" instead of "Neel" to this day.

In time the landing became a prosperous community, with stores, a hotel, a warehouse and other buildings. It thrived until modern highways and railroads replaced the paddlewheel riverboats as means of transportation. Today a boat landing, camping area and recreational park are maintained on the site.

The "Money Pond" still exists, although it is isolated from public access on a large tract of private property. If the old stories are true, then a pirate treasure remains there to this day, sinking deeper into the mud of the Chattahoochee River swamps with each passing year.

Although, William Augustus Bowles died in a Spanish prison, his legend lives on in Florida to this day. His piratical career is celebrated each year at the Billy Bowlegs Festival. A marker interpreting some elements of his life has been placed at St. George Island State Park, where he was shipwrecked in 1799. His attack on the Spanish fort at St. Marks is recounted at Florida's San Marcos de Apalache State Historic Park. The "Hickory Ground," where he was captured while attending a Creek Council, is today's Fort Toulouse/Jackson Historic Park in Wetumpka, Alabama (near Montgomery).

Figure 15: Alligators are among the modern inhabitants of Boynton Island

**Figure 16: In addition to its legendary "Ghost," Boynton Island was
a reported home of Two-Toed Tom**

Chapter Six

The "Fiddling Ghost" of Boynton Island

Ghost stories are important fixtures in the culture and history of Southern communities. As the chapter on the Ghost of Bellamy Bridge demonstrated, they usually have some basis in historical fact, even if the modern version has strayed a bit from the truth.

Unfortunately, many wonderful stories have faded away in recent years. The advent of computers, cable television and video in all forms has reduced our society's interest in old-fashioned story telling. Progress, of course, always means change, but unfortunately it often comes at a great price. Tall tales have become an endangered species.

In the case of Washington County, Florida, however, a number of fascinating stories have survived. They come to us largely thanks to the lifetime work of the late E.W. Carswell. A prominent Northwest Florida historian and folklorist, Judge Carswell made invaluable contributions to the preservation of the region's heritage.

He shared the story of the "fiddling ghost of Boynton Island" with me while we were working on his outstanding book, *Washington - Florida's Twelfth County*, during the late 1980s. The legend has long fascinated me so I decided to explore its roots. The result is the story that follows.

Even during the daylight, Boynton Island is a dark and mysterious place. Cypress trees and other hardwoods cast long shadows over the swamplands. The island is one of the supposed haunts of the legendary Northwest Florida and South Alabama monster, Two-Toed Tom. It also is near the spot where researchers from Auburn University recently announced the probable discovery of the Ivory-billed Woodpecker, long thought to be extinct.

The island itself, in fact, was formed by an anomaly of nature. Holmes Creek, flowing down from the northeast, enters the Choctawhatchee River at the foot of the island. Because the Choctawhatchee flows with a higher volume than Holmes Creek, it deposits much more sediment as it makes its way down from the red clay hills of Alabama to the Gulf of Mexico. As a result, the water of the Choctawhatchee runs at a higher elevation than that of the creek. Since water has a way of flowing downhill, a natural cut formed between the two streams as the Choctawhatchee River forced its way through solid earth to unite with Holmes Creek. The resulting piece of land, formed by the natural cut on the north and the confluence of the two streams on the south, is Boynton Island.

Two Egg, Florida

The name has been in use for a long time. Confederate enlistment papers from the War Between the States show that area men joined the Confederate army nearby at a place called Boynton Bluff.

The name Boynton may or may not be a corruption of either Boyington or Bowington. Two early settlers with similar names showed up on census records for the area in 1850 and 1860, but their names were spelled in different ways in different documents.

Haywood Boyington, listed as a 23-year-old man from Alabama, appeared on the 1850 census as the head of a family that included his wife, a 17-year-old woman who appears to have been his sister, and two young girls, evidently his daughters. He was no longer listed in the area by the time of the 1860 census, but another member of the family appears to have taken his place.

Moses Bowington, also from Alabama, was listed as a farmer on the 1860 roll. He was shown as living with 46-year-old Rhoda Bowington, 3-year-old George Bowington and 15-year-old Nancy J. Register. Three years later this same individual entered the Confederate service under the name Moses Boynton. He enlisted at the Cowford, a prominent early landmark a few miles south of Boynton Island near today's Ebro. After serving only a few months with Company C of the 11th Florida Infantry, however, he was dropped from the rolls. The records are silent as to the reason for his discharge.

What is known, however, is that during the last two years of the war, not long after Boynton left the service, Boynton Island became known as the hideout of a notorious group of men who survived by raiding the homes and farms of local citizens.

These groups or "gangs" were formed primarily by Confederate deserters and Southern Unionists. Some banded together for the sake of self-defense while they tried to make their way through to the Union lines. Others viewed the disintegrating situation near the end of the war as an opportunity to rob and plunder. Some did both. Among this latter group was a powerful gang headed by a man named Jim Ward.

A Confederate deserter, Ward set up headquarters on Boynton Island and recruited a gang of like-minded men. Together they terrorized much of the Choctawhatchee River valley, raiding farms and homesteads, carrying off supplies and stealing valuables. It was Ward's gang that attacked the Coffee County, Alabama, town of Elba on the morning of September 3, 1863. After burning the courthouse to destroy Confederate conscription or draft records, Ward and his men battled a local militia unit before setting fire to the bridge over the Pea River and escaping back into the swamps. Four militiamen were killed and two of Ward's men captured. Neither of the prisoners survived long. One, John Clark, was shot while trying to escape. The other was hanged. In retaliation, Ward shot a man named Columbus Holley through the window of his home.

Although Ward joined the Union army's 1st Florida U.S. Cavalry on March 24, 1864, he deserted this unit just four months later and spent the rest of the war hiding from both sides and launching raids from his hideout on Boynton Island. Legend holds that he assembled a considerable cache of valuables there, burying them around the island in spots known only to him. After the war, Ward lived nearby in Walton County and it was said that when he needed money, he would disappear into the swamps around Boynton Island and reappear with a handful of shiny gold coins.

What relationship Moses Boynton (or Boyington) had with these men is not known, but there must have at least been contact since they all lived in such a remote and isolated area. Perhaps he maintained a tenuous truce with Ward and his men, since local residents do not seem to have harbored hostility toward Boynton and his family nor does the family seemed to have been targeted by the raiders.

After the war, a sawmill industry developed at Choctawhatchee Bay and Moses and his son, Raymond, engaged in felling cypress timber to float downstream to the mills. They branded their name, "Boyington," on one end of each log before floating them downstream to be sawed into lumber.

Moses was known by others along the river as a man who enjoyed a good time. He played the fiddle and was said to be one of the best dance callers in the region. At night, the large Boyington home was often brightly illuminated. Friends, family and neighbors gathered there for food and dancing, often joined by the men from the logging camps up and down the river. These activities were well known along the Choctawhatchee and the sounds of the parties and music could often be heard for miles through the swamps surrounding Boynton Island.

After Moses passed away, his old log and frame house was abandoned. Or was it? Loggers camping at nearby Boynton Landing soon began to spread word that strange noises could be heard from the Boyington house late in the night. Lights were seen in the swamp and someone could be heard calling dances over the sound of a fiddle. News quickly spread that the ghost of old Moses Boyington had come back from the dead, along with a whole troop of dancing spirits.

For as long as the old house stood, locals avoided the area after dark. Tales of Moses Boyington and his dancing guests became legendary in the area. The dark and foreboding setting of the island added mysterious appeal to the story, especially as the old house slowly collapsed beneath shrouds of Spanish moss and the shadows of cypress trees. There is some disagreement as to whether the house finally collapsed on its own or burned in a fire, but either way it is gone now. The heavy timbering along the river came to an end as well. The story slowly faded, but no one can really say whether this is because the "fiddling ghost" of Moses Boyington stopped playing or simply because there was no longer anyone there to hear the music.

Figure 17: Northwest Florida Swamp

Figure 18: Chipola River Swamp

Chapter Seven

The West Florida Swamp Booger (Bigfoot)

Northwest Florida is known for its white sand beaches and blue Gulf waters, but these represent only the spectacular fringe of a special and beautiful area. Some of the South's most extensive forests and wetlands can be found here, stretching for mile upon mile through the valleys of the Apalachicola, Chipola, Choctawhatchee and other rivers. This region is unique with plants and animals that can be found nowhere else in the world. The torreya and Florida yew, for example, grow on the high bluffs and ravines along the Apalachicola and researchers have recently spotted the supposedly long-extinct Ivory-billed Woodpecker on the Choctawhatchee. But there may be something else living in these swamps, something that defies the imagination.

A surprisingly long list of eyewitnesses claims to have seen an unusual creature in the more remote areas of Northwest Florida. It is called by a variety of names. In South Florida, for example, people call it the skunk ape. In Arkansas, it is the Fouke Monster and in the mountains of the Pacific Northwest it is Sasquatch. Most people simply call it Bigfoot, but in Northwest Florida it best known as the "Swamp Booger."

The Swamp Booger has been part of the cultural landscape of Northwest Florida for many years. When early Scottish settlers first arrived in Walton County, the local Euchee Indians told them stories of a strange creature that inhabited a swampy area. The Euchee became alarmed when they learned the new settlers used wooden coffins to bury the remains of their dead. They believed this would allow the dead to come back as creatures like the one in the swamp. The early settlers preserved the Euchee legend by naming the swamp "Booger Bay."

Such stories are common in Native American culture and those who believe in the existence of Bigfoot have made much of them. It is worth noting, however, that there is anthropological evidence that early Native Americans were fascinated by the hairy faces and bodies of the European explorers who first encountered them. Legends of these "hairy men" could have evolved into tales of large, hairy creatures as they were repeated over the centuries.

One thing that sets the legendary Swamp Booger apart from stories about other such creatures is that it is said to be carnivorous. In the mid-1980s the creature attracted considerable attention after something broke into numerous hog pens along the Choctawhatchee River and its tributaries, slaughtering hogs by the dozen. Eyewitnesses reported seeing a massive hairy creature in the area and before long someone showed up with plaster casts of giant footprints.

Two Egg, Florida

Although the hog killings finally stopped, similar stories continue to be told. In Jackson County, one witness claimed that something was raiding her family's chicken coop and leaving the chickens dead with huge bites missing from their carcasses. Another witness in Walton County blamed a Swamp Booger for stealing an entire deer. There also have been reports of creatures confronting cars, scaring hunters, of strange noises in the night and of unbearable smells coming from the areas where they have been seen or heard.

There have been many explanations for such sightings. Bears frequent many of the areas where the Swamp Booger has been seen and certainly could be responsible for some of the reports. Coyotes and other animals could easily be responsible for the attacks on chicken coops and hog pens, Perhaps the most intriguing possibility, at least for sightings through much of the 20th century, is that a large ape really could have been roaming parts of the region.

During the early 1900s, an area newspaper published a fascinating story about the escape of a live, male gorilla from a ship off the Walton County coast. The gorilla had been brought back from Africa by the ship's captain, who had visions of selling or exhibiting him for a profit. As the vessel was coasting for Pensacola, however, the large primate caught sight of the shoreline and became extremely agitated. Before the crew could do anything to bring him under control, he broke free from his cage and rampaged about the deck. After thoroughly terrifying the sailors, the gorilla finally mounted one of the rails and stood staring across the water at the shore. Gathering sufficient nerve, one of the crew finally crept up behind him and pushed the startled animal overboard. He was last seen swimming away, heading for the beach.

No one really knows what became of the gorilla. These animals have an average lifespan of between 30 and 50 years, so he undoubtedly died decades ago. It is entirely possible, however, that he could have been responsible for unexplained sightings in the region for many years. Curiously, distressed gorillas are known to give off a pungent body odor. Horrendous smells are often coupled with stories of Swamp Booger sightings.

Whatever the truth behind the sightings, they have been a popular part of Northwest Florida folklore for many years and the stories show no signs of letting up.

Figure 19: Eden Gardens, near where the Gorilla swam to shore.

Figure 20: Wilderness areas like this are known for "Swamp Booger" sightings.

Figure 21: Spectacular Formations at Florida Caverns State Park

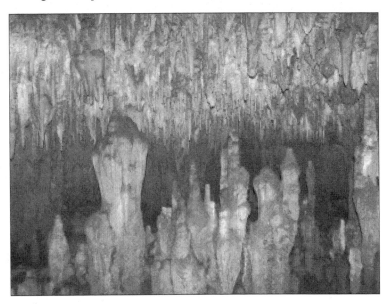

Figure 22: Inside the Tour Cave at Florida Caverns State Park

Chapter Eight

Florida's Underground Wonderland

For tens of thousands of years, water has slowly eaten away at the limestone or karst topography of Jackson County, leaving hundreds of caves and caverns ranging in size from tiny to magnificent. Beautiful and mysterious places, these underground passages and chambers have spawned a variety of legends and stories, some of them true and some not.

A personal favorite was recorded by J. Randal Stanley in his original *History of Jackson County*. That story holds that early settlers were exploring the Natural Bridge cavern at what is now Florida Caverns State Park when a wall unexpectedly collapsed. When the dust cleared, an ancient Spaniard emerged, like Rip Van Winkle, claiming that he had been asleep in the cave for many years.

That story, obviously, is not true, but many other legends do have foundations in fact. Native Americans used the caves as shelters and hiding places, while citizens and slaves hid in them during the Battle of Marianna. One is even said to rise so close to the surface beneath the Jackson County Courthouse that a rescue party searching for lost children once heard courtroom activity from above. The legendary flooded caves at Blue Springs and Merritt's Mill Pond have claimed many lives through the years.

Human use of the caves dates back many centuries. Archaeologists working at both Florida Caverns State Park and Waddell's Mill Pond have found considerable evidence for early use of caves by Native Americans. A cave at the state park, in fact, was so pristine that footprints left centuries ago were still visible on the floor. Without rain and wind to wipe them away, these traces of ancient people were as well-preserved as if they had been left yesterday. Similarly, the partially-collapsed cavern at Waddell's Mill Pond revealed numerous artifacts and even the burial place of a small child.

The first Spanish to settle in the region, missionaries who came west from what is now Tallahassee to convert the Chacato or Chatot people living along and west of the upper Chipola River, made note of and explored the caves. A Franciscan priest, Fray Rodrigo de la Barreda, noted the caves around Blue Springs and recorded that they were often used by Native American hunters.

Fray Rodrigo and a fellow missionary, Fray Miguel de Valverde, established two missions west of the Chipola in 1674. One of these, San Nicolas de Tolentino, stood at the mouth of a magnificent cave. Fray Rodrigo described this cavern when he revisited the site in 1693:

Two Egg, Florida

> *Here we spent the night in the hollow of such a beautiful and unusual rock that I can state positively that more than 200 men could be lodged most comfortably within it; inside there is a brook which gushes from the living rock. It has plenty of light and height with three apertures buttressed by stonework of unusual natural architecture. Around it are level plots of ground, groves of trees and pine woods, all of which are delightful.*

The friar was mostly likely describing Rock Arch Cave about three miles northwest of Marianna. Of all the many caves and caverns in the region, this is the one that most closely resembles the Spanish account. Things did not go well here for the Franciscans. They took away all but one of a local chief's multiple wives as part of their effort to convert him to Christianity. He responded by inciting a revolt that drove the friars from Chacato territory in 1675.

Rock Arch Cave, however, remained a curiosity for other early travelers. John Lee Williams, the early historian and explorer who helped picked the site for Florida's capital city, described it in his 1827 *View of West Florida*:

> *The Arch cave is situation near the public road, about three miles west of the ferries on Chapola River, in Jackson County. It opens, to the east, an aperture under a vast limestone rock; about five feet high, and thirty feet wide. This passage descends gently, for three or four rods; the cavern then opens, to the extent of a hundred feet wide, and fifty feet high. A deep channel, of transparent water, skirts the south side, for some distance; it then breaks off in wells, and finally disappears altogether.*

The Williams account goes on to describe the myriad of passages that lead off from the large cavern or entry chamber.

The Rock Arch Cave is just one of many in Jackson County with rich histories. The Natural Bridge or "Indian" Cave at Florida Caverns State Park was supposedly used as a hiding place by Native Americans when Andrew Jackson's army marched across the county during the First Seminole War. No one really knows whether this actually happened. Based on the account of Captain Hugh Young, Jackson's topographer, the army did march past the entrance of the cave on its way from the Apalachicola River to Pensacola. There is no authentication, however, that Creek or Seminole warriors were hiding in the vicinity.

Legend also holds that citizens and slaves hid in the cave during the Battle of Marianna. The Natural Bridge Cave was well known at that time and the story may be true, but none of the eyewitness accounts confirm it. A similar story is told of a large cave that lies beneath the city of Marianna itself. The now-sealed entrance to this cavern is on the bank of the Chipola River just north of the U.S. 90 bridge. The cave is sealed because local children loved to explore it, often losing their way and having to be rescued by search parties. One such party claimed to have heard courtroom activity from above during a search and rescue expedition. This probably was a bit of a stretch, but the cave is indeed extensive.

The most famous of the caves in Jackson County, of course, are those now open to the public at Florida Caverns State Park. As the story is told thousands of times by guides, the tour cave at the park was discovered after a tree blew over. The hole left by its roots opened into a large room and further exploration revealed a vast cavern. Initially there were plans to make the Caverns a private attraction, but during the 1930s title to the property was transferred and Florida's seventh state park was created. The nation was then in the depths of the Great Depression and as part of President Franklin Roosevelt's New Deal a camp of Civilian Conservation Corps (CCC) workers was established at the park. The CCC crews excavated passages through the caverns, moving tons of earth and rock to create the paths that visitors now use to see the spectacular rooms and formations. The park opened to the public in 1942.

Today Florida Caverns State Park is one of the state's most beautiful and unique attractions. The caves offer visitors a chance to experience a part of Florida that otherwise few would ever see. In addition, the park includes nature and equestrian trails, campgrounds, picnic areas, a canoe launch and swimming in the clear, cold waters of Blue Hole Spring.

For those who aren't quite up to the challenge of a walking tour through the main caverns, a shorter "tunnel cave" can be explored on one of the park's nature trails. The entrances to other caves and a rock shelter once used by Native American hunters can also be seen from the trails.

One of Jackson County's other favorite attractions, Blue Springs, is the site of one of the deepest series of underwater caverns in the world. The submerged caves are extremely dangerous and have claimed many lives over the years, but professional explorers have mapped them to a great distance and depth. The entrance to the cave can be seen from the diving platform at Blue Springs Recreation Area, which is open during the summer season. The crystal clear water provides a phenomenal view of the underwater ravine and cave opening, especially first thing in the morning before swimmers stir up the water.

Figure 23: Andrew Jackson, photographed late in life.

Figure 24: The Chipola River as seen from the Natural Bridge

Chapter Nine

Andrew Jackson and the Natural Bridge

One of Jackson County's oldest legends revolves around the passage of Andrew Jackson's army through the Chipola River country during the First Seminole War of 1817-1818. As the story goes, Jackson had completed a hard-driving raid through Middle Florida and had just returned to Fort Gadsden on the Apalachicola River when he learned that Spanish authorities in Pensacola were sheltering and supplying Creek and Seminole warriors. Outraged, "Old Hickory" determined to seize the city and started off with an army of over 1,000 men.

Marching north from Fort Gadsden, Jackson crossed the Apalachicola at Ocheese Bluff in what is now Calhoun County. From there, he turned northwest to Blue Spring and finally the Natural Bridge of the Chipola River. Here, according to legend, an unusual incident took place.

As the army advanced, it was said to have been marching in two columns. The first, under Jackson himself, was well-guided by an area chief named Lafarka or John Blunt, the man for whom modern-day Blountstown is named. Lafarka guided Jackson's column across the Natural Bridge at Florida Caverns State Park, supposedly under the watchful eyes of Native American warriors who were hiding in a nearby cave. Since the Chipola flows underground at this point, it is said that Jackson never knew he had crossed a river.

The other column of the army, however, was not so fortunate. Legend holds that these men had to construct rafts to get across and were so delayed in linking up with Jackson that the general was in an explosive mood by the time they arrived. Known for his volatile personality, "Old Hickory" flew into a rage. When his subordinates tried to explain they were delayed by having to cross a river, he supposedly became even angrier for he had seen no river at all. It was not until Lafarka explained the situation that Jackson could be calmed.

It is the only real legend associated with Jackson in the county that bears his name, but unfortunately it appears to be little more than one of many tall tales that have been handed down about the man. Jackson's topographer, Captain Hugh Young, prepared a meticulous account of the general's march through Florida, and while he mentions the natural bridge incident, he describes it as happening at a natural bridge between St. Marks and the Suwannee River, not at the Natural Bridge of the Chipola. Apparently over time the story was transferred from one location to another.

Although the story of the Natural Bridge incident was not true, Young's account of Andrew Jackson's march through what is now Jackson County provides a fascinating early look at the area. Having crossed the Apalachicola River, Jackson set out from Ocheese Bluff on March 10, 1818, at the head of an army of 1,092 men. The route was described by Young as being through good country and the soldiers camped for the night at Blue Spring, which the captain called the "Big Spring." He described it as, "forty yards in diameter and of considerable depth with a rock bottom and a clean and rapid current."

On the morning of March 11, 1818, the army continued its march to the northwest and Young's account leaves no doubt that they knew they were marching across a natural bridge when they reached the Chipola:

> *The Natural Bridge is in the center of a large swamp and appears to be a deposit of earth on a raft or some similar obstruction. The passage is narrow and the creek, with a rapid current is visible both above and below.*

Young, of course, was wrong about the formation of the Natural Bridge. The river sinks into a limestone passage here and flows underground for a short distance before rising back to the surface. During the 19th century, loggers dug a canal across the top of the feature to allow them to float timber across to a mill downstream, taking away some of the unique appearance of the bridge.

The Natural Bridge of the Chipola is now preserved as part of Florida Caverns State Park. It lies on the main road connecting the Visitor Center and picnic areas with Blue Hole Spring. A marker at a canoe launch by the sink provides a brief history of Andrew Jackson's march through the area, an event that had great significance in the future of Florida. By demonstrating that Spain was unable to defend its colony, Jackson's 1818 invasion set the stage for the transfer of Florida to the United States just three years later. Many of the men in his army were so impressed by the Chipola River country that they returned to settle the region in the coming years. The march through Northwest Florida was the final act in a military career that propelled Jackson first to the governorship of Florida and finally to the Presidency of the United States. Jackson County bears his name.

Other sites associated with the First Seminole War can also be visited in Florida. Principal among these is Fort Gadsden, where Jackson began the march that took him across the Natural Bridge of the Chipola. The earthworks of the old fort still remain and can be seen, along with interpretive displays and spectacular views of the Apalachicola River, at Fort Gadsden Historic Site. The park is located in the Apalachicola National Forest just south of Sumatra.

Fort St. Marks, where Jackson captured the Creek Prophet Josiah Francis and the alleged British agent Alexander Arbuthnot is also preserved. Located on the grounds of the San Marcos de Apalache State Historic Park at St. Marks, Florida, the ruins of the old fort can be seen. A museum on the grounds provides more information on Jackson's capture of the fort and the First Seminole War. Additional exhibits are available nearby in Tallahassee at the Museum of Florida

Chapter Nine

History in the R.A. Gray Building adjacent to the capitol complex. The building also contains the state archives and library.

Fort Barrancas, another Spanish fort attacked by Jackson at the conclusion of his West Florida campaign, is now part of Gulf Islands National Seashore. Located at the Pensacola Naval Air Station, the fort and its grounds are maintained by the National Park Service and are open daily for public tour. A museum on the grounds provides additional detail and one of the two fortifications still standing in the park was there during Jackson's attack.

Figure 25: The Earthworks of Fort Gadsden, Apalachicola National Forest

Figure 26: Crest of the Waterfall, Falling Waters State Park

Figure 27: Oil well site, Falling Waters State Park

Chapter Ten

The Washington County Volcano

Falling Waters Hill, near Chipley in Washington County, is the focal point of several of Northwest Florida's most unusual legends. Now the centerpiece of Falling Waters State Park, the hill takes its name from an unusual waterfall that tumbles over a rocky ledge and into a cylindrical lime sink. The waterfall alone makes the hill one of Florida's most unique natural features, but if an old story is to be believed, it also hides Florida's only volcano.

The story comes from an old document that purports to be a translation of the centuries' old account of an early Spanish explorer named Jose Matanzas. It begins with a claim that Matanzas was captured by Indians while exploring on the upper Apalachicola River not long after the settlement of St. Augustine in 1565. He says he remained among them for three years and that during this time, hunters began to come in with stories of a place where the earth was on fire. Matanzas told the Native American hunters of Mt. Vesuvious in Italy and they insisted he go with them to see the place in hopes that he might be able to explain it.

Leaving from a high bluff on the east side of the Apalachicola, they traveled for two days. On the second night, they saw a "great flash that seemed to me to be the lightning from a cloud." The hunter who was guiding him told the Spaniard that they were on "dangerous earth." Soon, they were able to feel the earth trembling.

At 11 o'clock the next morning, the party found themselves surrounded by a "great fog of smoke" that smelled like burning leather. Before long they reached the source of the smoke:

> *...Soon we got to the fire, and it was a liquid running down a hollow slough on fire. The red liquid was oozing out of a hill top of rocks in several places, and there seemed to be a deadly gas in the air. We could not go on top of the hill. This gas made us faintly. So we camped a mile north that night, and some time near the middle of the night a great explosion occurred on this hill. For more than an hour it seemed that the whole elements were on fire, and a great hissing sound on the hill. Soon everything hushed and all was quiet and light of the fire died down.*

The next morning the party went back up to the hill and found that the red liquid was still running down its east and west sides. Suddenly another explosion took place and a flash of deadly gas "rolled up to the Heavens for a short while and all got quiet." Matanzas claimed that large sand stones came out of the hill with each explosion, along with the burning liquid and some kind of white slush.

It is a colorful tale, but almost certainly not true. Falling Waters Hill is of karst topography and is riddled with sinks and caves. This is not the type of geology that produces volcanoes. It is also worth noting that Matanzas gives distances in miles, while real Spanish documents of the time period used leagues.

But if the story is not true, what was the purpose in creating it? The answer may rest in rumors that the area is rich in oil. In 1919 a wildcat operation drilled one of the first oil wells in Florida on Falling Waters Hill. There was speculation by promoters of the well that some of the rocks found there had been formed from oil-bearing material. It is highly suspicious that the purported Matanzas account first appeared at about this same time. Could it have been propaganda to help encourage investment in the drilling effort? Stranger things have happened.

The oil well did not produce a gusher, but it was one of the most significant wells drilled in Florida prior to 1954. The drillers went past 3,900 feet and did succeed in striking a gas pocket, but they never hit oil in commercial quantities. The project was abandoned and all that remains today is a capped metal pipe and slight indentation in the earth.

Ironically, it was this abandoned well that helped open the door for the creation of Falling Waters State Park. The Chipley Kiwanis Club had been working for several years to create a park around the waterfall, but the state was not inclined to buy the land and the owner, International Paper Company, had no desire to sell. Unexpectedly, though, a cow fell into a sludge pit left over from the drilling operation. The animal was rescued, but newspaper coverage of the event focused on the open pits, deep sinks and dangerous caves in the area. Managers for the paper company immediately recognized they could face serious liability if anyone was hurt on the property, so they donated 7.8 acres atop Falling Waters Hill to Washington County.

The donation was followed by other property exchanges and in 1961 the Florida State Legislature appropriated funding to begin construction of Falling Waters State Park. The park today is a true jewel. Located atop the picturesque hill, it offers walking trails and boardwalks, one of which leads down into the primary sink to provide visitors with a spectacular view of the 73-foot waterfall. There are also picnic areas, a swimming lake and campgrounds as well as other facilities.

Figure 28: Walkway to Waterfall, Falling Waters State Park

Figure 29: Pathway Descending into Falling Waters Sink

Figure 30: Ivory-billed Woodpeckers painted by John James Audubon

Chapter Eleven

The Ivory-billed Woodpecker

For thousands of years, a marvelous bird inhabited the forests of the Choctawhatchee, Chipola and Apalachicola Rivers in Northwest Florida. It was called the Ivory-billed Woodpecker and it was one of the most magnificent sights ever seen not only in the region, but in America.

The Ivory-billed was a magical bird with a wing-span of as much as 30-31 inches. The bills of the bird were once used as important trade items by Native Americans and archaeologists have found their skulls at sites far outside of their historical range. Perhaps the Native American fascination with the birds came from their unique size and beauty. They were the third-largest woodpeckers in the world and the largest north of Mexico. The birds were also recreated in early Native American effigy art which implies they may have had ceremonial significance.

The unique woodpeckers survived in eastern North America for thousands of years. Their primary habitat was in the vast old growth pine forests of the coastal plains. Unfortunately, the forest growth that was so attractive to the Ivory-billed also was of great economic significance to early settlers and industrialists. As the forest industry harvested the vast old forests of the Deep South, the habitat of the bird was significantly reduced. By the 1880s sightings of the birds were rare and as the timber industries accelerated to supply the military needs of America during World Wars I and II, most experts came to believe that the Ivory-billed had been wiped out.

Experts, however, are not always the people who know best. In the surviving old-growth timber along the Apalachicola, Chipola and Choctawhatchee Rivers, hunters and fishers kept reporting sightings of the magnificent birds. Unfortunately, the experts did not believe them. The last official sighting of an Ivory-billed was in 1944 and new reports from the swamps of Northwest Florida were greeted with skepticism and sometimes even downright ridicule.

Occasionally someone conducted an actual search and the results were usually encouraging. In 1951-1952, for example, Whitney Eastman reported finding Ivory-billed Woodpeckers still living along the Chipola River in Calhoun County. Researcher John V. Dennis visited the same area in 1951 and reported hearing the unique calls of the birds, although he did not actually see one. Other researchers, however, could not substantiate the sightings and they were largely forgotten.

Two Egg, Florida

Local residents, though, continued to see them. In the 1970s and 80s, a number of sightings were reported by outdoorsmen along the Chipola River in Jackson County, but experts declined to investigate and declared that the Ivory-billed was extinct. Fortunately, other efforts resulted in the preservation of much of the natural habitat along the rivers of Northwest Florida. The Northwest Florida Water Management District, for example, purchased thousands of acres of land along the Chipola River and joined with other organizations to protect natural habitat along both the Choctawhatchee and Apalachicola. In doing so, these organizations may well have helped save a species.

Then, the possible sighting and video-taping of an Ivory-billed in eastern Arkansas in 2004 created a burst of fascination with the birds. The U.S. Fish and Wildlife Service launched immediate efforts to protect the possible birds in Arkansas, but thus far no one has been able to confirm the sightings there.

The Arkansas sighting, however, prompted curious researchers from Auburn University to revisit the areas in Northwest Florida where people have been seeing the birds all along. As they were paddling kayaks through the swamps of the Choctawatchee River, a magnificent Ivory-billed suddenly swept down from the trees and flew directly above the head of researcher Geoffrey Hill. Since then, the Auburn investigators have spotted Ivory-billed Woodpeckers 14 times along the Choctawhatchee and have recorded sounds matching their acoustics more than 40 times. They have also made another 300 recordings of what they believe are sounds created by the woodpeckers, including the unique "double knock" hammering sound they make and their "kent, kent, kent" calls.

More research is underway and it now seems likely that sightings will soon be verified on other river systems in the area, particularly the Chipola and Apalachicola. For sixty years local outdoorsmen have maintained that the Ivory-billed was still there and even though their sightings had been written off as cases of mistaken identity and folklore, in the end they can smile about it. Not only were they right all along, but now even the experts are admitting that Northwest Florida could prove to be the "Shangri-la" of the Ivory-billed Woodpecker.

The search for the Ivory-billed is now spreading throughout the South and many experts believe it is just a matter of time before conclusive proof of their survival will be found.

Figure 31: Pine Forests of Northwest Florida

Figure 32: Ivory-billed Woodpecker habitat in Northwest Florida

Figure 33: 19th Century drawing of Milly Francis pleading for McKrimmon's Life

Figure 34: Milly Francis Memorial at San Marcos de Apalache

Chapter Twelve

The Story of Milly Francis

Although her legend has faded some over the years, Milly Francis was one of the most remarkable women in American history. The daughter of the Creek Prophet Josiah Francis, she is perhaps best remembered as the "Creek Pocahontas." Many believe that Millie is the Native American woman who appears on the Great Seal of the State of Florida.

The story of Milly Francis revolves around an incident that took place during the First Seminole War of 1817-1818. Troops under Andrew Jackson had marched down the east bank of the Apalachicola River and established a new outpost, Fort Gadsden, on the site of an earlier British fort. Unaware that Native American scouts were hovering around the fort, a young Georgia militiaman named Duncan McKrimmon wandered off in search of a good fishing hole. He had not gone far when he was taken prisoner by a group of warriors loyal to Josiah Francis.

The Prophet Francis had been one of the leaders of the "Red Stick" movement, a religious movement among the Creeks tied to the teachings of the Shawnee Prophet Tenskwatawa and his brother, Tecumseh. After the Red Sticks were defeated at the Battle of Horseshoe Bend, Alabama, in March of 1814, Francis and thousands of his followers fled across the line into Spanish Florida. By the time of Jackson's 1818 invasion of Florida, the Prophet was living in a village on the east bank of the Wakulla River near the Spanish fort of San Marcos de Apalache.

McKrimmon was taken to this village by his captors, who tied him naked to a pole and prepared to torture him to death. It was a pathetic scene and the young daughter of the Prophet, Milly, took pity on the soldier and pleaded with her father to spare his life. Francis responded that he had no power over the situation and that Milly should talk with the warrior who had captured McKrimmon. She went immediately to this warrior, who told her that he intended to execute McKrimmon in the Creek fashion to atone for the life of his sister who had been killed in the Red Stick war. Milly reasoned with him that slaying the young Georgian would not bring back his lost sister, also pointing out that McKrimmon was barely more than a boy and not fit to be slain as a warrior. The Red Stick considered the matter and agreed to release McKrimmon on the condition that the militiaman's head be shaved and that he live permanently with Francis and his people.

Anxious to save his life, McKrimmon quickly agreed to the conditions and was released after the warriors shaved his head in the Creek fashion. He remained in the village briefly before being turned over to the Spanish commandant at San Marcos to be held as a prisoner. The Spanish treated him kindly and allowed him freedom to roam the fort at will, but warned him they could not release him without facing the wrath of the Prophet and his warriors. Only a few days passed, however, before Jackson's army appeared outside the fort and, in a sudden rush, stormed the gates and took possession of the works.

In the meantime, a U.S. ship had sailed up the St. Marks River flying a British flag. Believing it to be long-awaited supplies, the Prophet Francis and another chief had paddled out in a canoe to greet the vessel. Instead, they were taken prisoner and turned over to Jackson after he seized the fort. Seeing McKrimmon, Francis asked that he intercede to save his life but McKrimmon is said to have responded that he owed his life to Milly and to Milly alone. The Prophet was hanged by Jackson's order.

McKrimmon rejoined his regiment and took part in the rest of the campaign, but the story holds that he later returned to Florida and offered his hand in marriage to Milly. There are several stories as to what happened next. One holds that she accepted the offer and lived out the rest of her life with McKrimmon on a farm near Suwannee Old Town. Others, however, conclude that she turned him down and spent the rest of her days with her own people. It has also been said that her name was not Milly at all, but Malee, a Creek name that signified something along the line of "Morning Dove."

The real story of Milly Francis is actually much more compelling than any of the legends. Born in Alabama in around 1813, she was indeed one of the daughters of the Prophet Francis. Since all of the members of the Prophet's family had English names, there is no reason to doubt that Milly was her real name. It was unquestionably the name she used later in life following her conversion to Christianity.

The incident involving McKrimmon was real. It first appeared in the pages of Milledgeville *Journal* on November 2, 1818, shortly after the end of the war:

> *The ruthless savages, having shaved his head and reduced his body to a state of nudity, formed themselves into a circle, and danced around him some hours, yelling all the while most horribly. The youngest daughter of the Prophet (who is about fifteen years of age and represented by officers of the army we have conversed with to be a woman very superior to her associates) was sad and silent the whole time – she participated not in the general joy, but was evidently, even to the affrighted prisoner, much pained at the savage scene she was compelled to witness. When the fatal tomahawk was raised to terminate forever the mortal existence of the unfortunate McKrimmon – at that critical, that awful moment, Milly Francis, like an angel of Mercy, placed herself between it and death, resolutely bidding the astonished executioner, if he thirsted for human blood to shed hers.*

Chapter Twelve

Following the execution of her father, Milly was with the rest of her people when they surrendered to American officials at San Marcos, now called St. Marks. They were ordered back to the Creek Nation in Alabama and Georgia by way of Fort Gadsden and reached that fort in a destitute condition. Lieutenant Colonel Matthew Arbuckle, the commanding officer there, noted their arrival in a report to Andrew Jackson, who by now had moved west of the Apalachicola River and captured Pensacola. The story continued in the pages of the Milledgeville *Journal*:

> *Now, the fortune of war has placed her in the power of the white people – she arrived at Fort Gadsden not long since, with a number of others that had surrendered, in a starving condition. We are gratified to learn that a proper respect for her virtues induced the commanding officer, Colonel Arbuckle, to relieve her immediate wants. McKrimmon appears to have a due sense of the obligation he owes the woman who saved his life at the hazard of her own – he left town last week to seek her, and as far as may be in his power to alleviate her misfortunes. It is also his firm determination, we understand, if she will consent, to make her his wife, and reside provided he an prevail on her to do so, within the settled parts of Georgia.*

Spellbound by the story, the citizens of Milledgeville took up a collection to assist Milly and sent it to Colonel Arbuckle at Fort Gadsden. By December 1, 1818, the colonel reported that Duncan McKrimmon had reached the fort and that his long-awaited second meeting with Milly Francis had taken place:

> *Milly…says she saved his life, or used such influence as she possessed to that effect, from feelings of humanity alone, and that she would have rendered the same service to any other white man similarly circumstanced. She is, therefore, not disposed to accept his offer of matrimony, which has been made as an acknowledgement of gratitude. The donation presented through me by the citizens of Milledgeville to Milly, has been delivered, and she manifested a considerable degree of thankfulness for their kindness.*

By this point of her life, Milly must have been more than slightly confused about the attitudes of the whites. She had been driven from her home in Alabama during the Creek War of 1813-1814, taken shelter in Florida, saved the life of a white soldier, seen her father executed at the end of a rope, subjected to near starvation and finally presented with gifts and a marriage proposal by the people she considered her enemies.

Two Egg, Florida

Milly returned with her family to the Creek Nation and settled in the town of Tuckabatchee on the Tallapoosa River. She married a warrior there, raised a family and lived in peace for the next twenty years. In 1836, however, her husband joined a force of Creek warriors who went to fight on the side of the United States against the Seminoles of Florida. He was killed on the battlefield and never returned. In the meantime, a faction of the Creeks also went to war and a conflict known as the Creek War of 1836 spread across parts of Alabama and Georgia. Most of the Tuckabatchee stayed out of the fight or fought on the side of the whites, but when the war ended they were rounded into concentration camps with the rest of their people and sent west on the Trail of Tears. Milly and her children, destitute and without a provider, were part of this forced march, traveling part of the way on foot and part by boat. They endured hunger and extreme conditions, but finally reached Little Rock, Arkansas, in December of 1836. Her passage there was noted by the editor of a local newspaper who wrote that she was surprised that people along the way had remembered the story of her saving McKrimmon and had shown her courtesy and helped in small ways.

The long column pushed on and entered the new Creek Nation in what is now Oklahoma in January of 1837. Hundreds had died along the way and their bones could be seen on the sides of the roads they took for many years to come.

Milly settled not far from Fort Gibson on the present site of Muskogee, Oklahoma. With help from others, she built a little cabin in the vicinity of today's Bacone College campus and once again started a new life. Life in the new nation was very tough. Food supplies were limited and sickness raged among the new arrivals. Slowly, however, the Creeks began to establish themselves in their new and strange country.

Baptist missionaries were active among the Native Americans during these early years and Milly was attracted by their efforts. She joined the church and was baptized into the Christian faith, a decision that probably would have shocked her father, who had led a nativistic revival among his people.

Milly's story might well have faded into obscurity after her arrival west of the Mississippi, but there was to be one more unique episode in her life.

During the winter of 1841-1842, Colonel Ethan A. Hitchcock was sent west to investigate allegations that the destitute people were being defrauded in their new homes. While at Fort Gibson, Hitchcock learned that Milly Francis was living nearby and immediately sought her out. He found her living in poverty in her small cabin.

Curious as to the truth of her unusual story, Hitchock asked Milly to share with him her own memories of the now famous event:

> *Milly began by saying that an elder sister and herself were*
> *playing on the bank of the river, when they heard a war-cry,*
> *which they understood to signify that a prisoner had been taken.*
> *They immediately went in the direction of the cry and found a*

white man, tied to a tree, and two young warriors, with their rifles, dancing around him preparatory to putting him to death, as was their right according to custom. She explained to me that in such cases the life of the prisoner is the in the hands of the captors – even the chiefs have no authority in the case. She was then but fifteen or sixteen years of age; 'the prisoner was a young man' said Milly, 'and seemed very much frightened and looked wildly around to see if anyone would help him. I thought it a pity that a young man like him should be put to death and I spoke to my father and told him it was a pity to kill him – for he had no head to go to war with' (meaning that he had been led off by others). 'My father told me,' continued Milly, 'that he could not save him, and advised me to speak to the Indians. I did so. One of them was very much enraged, saying he had lost two sisters in the war and would put the prisoner to death. I told him that it would not bring his sisters back to kill the young man, and so, talking to him for some time, I finally persuaded him, and he said that if the young man would agree to have his head shave, and dress like an Indian, and live among them, they would save his life.'

Milly told Hitchcock that she was very poor and had to work very hard just to survive. She had given birth over the intervening years to eight children, but only three still survived and they were too young to be of help to her.

The colonel was moved by her situation and recommended to Washington that the government take some steps to assist her and reduce her suffering. On June 17, 1844, the U.S. Congress approved a bill granting Milly a pension of $96 per year and, "a medal with appropriate devices thereon, of the value of not exceeding twenty dollars, as an additional testimonial of the gratitude of the United States." It was the first special medal of honor ever presented to a female recipient by the Congress of the United States.

It was not until May 7, 1848, nearly four years later, that news of the pension and medal finally reached the Creek Nation. The agent there, James Logan, sought out Milly to present it to her:

...I immediately visited her, and found her as I was informed, in dying circumstances and I regret to say in a most wretched condition. I immediately procured medical aid, & done all that was possible to alleviate her sufferings. I read your letter to her, (she comprehending English perfectly) and by which she was so highly elated, that I flattered myself she was recovering, but my hopes were fallacious, her disease was consumption.

Consumption is what we today call tuberculosis. Milly Francis died on May 19, 1848, "a Christian, devout member of the Baptist Church." She was buried near her home in a now-unmarked grave believed to be somewhere on or near the campus of Bacone College.

In her final hours she told Logan that, "at the time the act was rendered which saved the life of Capt. McKrimmon, she never expected any pecuniary reward, her family were rich, she did not require it. She had become very poor - & she was grateful for the notice taken of her by the Govt., etc."

In addition to the possibility that her image appears on the Great Seal of Florida, Milly Francis is memorialized at two other locations in the state. A plaque and stone boulder bear tribute to her at San Marcos de Apalache in St. Marks, a few miles from the site of Francis' village on the Wakulla River. A state marker telling her story can also be found at Fort Gadsden Historic Site in the Apalachicola National Forest, from which McKrimmon was captured in the spring of 1818.

In Oklahoma, Milly is a beloved figure. A stone monument on the grounds of Bacone College in Muskogee commemorates her life. The college stands on or near the site where Milly lived her final years and died. In nearby Fort Gibson, the Oklahoma Historical Society maintains the grounds of the old fort where the Trail of Tears came to an end. The original stockade has been reconstructed and it is possible to see the fort much as it appeared when Milly passed through.

The descendents of Milly Francis still live in Oklahoma, hundreds of miles away from the land that her father fought so fiercely to save.

Figure 35: Milly Francis Monument at Bacone College, Oklahoma

Figure 36: Fort Gibson, Oklahoma

Figure 37: The Bible of St. Luke's Episcopal Church

Figure 38: St. Luke's Episcopal Church, Site of the Battle of Marianna

Chapter Thirteen

The Bible of St. Luke's Episcopal Church

On September 27, 1864, a large force of Union soldiers attacked the Northwest Florida city of Marianna. It was the deepest penetration of Confederate Florida by Federal forces during the entire Civil War and resulted in an encounter so severe that some veteran participants described it as the most intense fight of the war. Remembered today as the Battle of Marianna, the engagement is memorialized by a monument and several markers. The most poignant memorial of the battle, however, is not written in stone or bronze, but on paper. A large 19th century Bible is carefully preserved in a case at St. Luke's Episcopal Church. While Bibles of its age are not all that rare, this one is the focus of an unusual and treasured Northwest Florida legend. *

During the final stages of the Battle of Marianna, after a portion of the Confederate forces had been pushed across the Chipola Rivers and others forced to abandon the fight, the last organized defenders withdrew into the yard surrounding St. Luke's and prepared to fall back deeper into town to continue their fight. A second column of Federal attackers came in behind them, however, and forced these men to make a desperate last stand among the graves of their ancestors. The churchyard was surrounded by wooden fence, which the defenders used as a makeshift fortification to keep their attackers at bay. Some took up positions in the church itself, firing from the windows at the Union soldiers who closed in from all sides.

Most of these men were not professional soldiers. They were storekeepers, doctors, teachers, schoolboys and attorneys who left their normal professions to take up arms that morning as part of the Marianna Home Guard. Their captain, Jesse Norwood, was a lawyer who had once served in the 5th Florida Cavalry. There were some veterans among their ranks. Some were men who had been wounded in larger battles and were now home on furlough to recover and others were Confederate cavalrymen who had been unhorsed earlier in the battle but had fallen in with Norwood's men and continued to fight.

The battle waged by Norwood's Home Guards at St. Luke's Church became a Florida legend. Union officers, in fact, were stunned by the level of resistance they were able to offer. When asked after the battle how a group of untrained volunteers could fight so well, a local doctor named Ethelred Philips replied that

---

* For a detailed account, please consider *The Battle of Marianna, Florida* by this author. More information is available at www.battleofmarianna.net.

they "were born to it." As he went on to explain, almost everyone in the area had grown up hunting and handling guns.

The Union general, Alexander Asboth, had been severely wounded earlier in the battle and by the time of the last stand in the churchyard, command of the Federal soldiers had fallen to Colonel L.L. Zulavsky of the 82nd U.S. Colored Infantry. A former Hungarian freedom fighter and nephew of the noted European revolutionary Lajos Kossuth, Zulavsky knew that the fight must be brought to a close. He brought up two companies of men from the 82nd and 86th U.S. Colored Infantries (U.S.C.I.) and had them charge the churchyard. The scene was described in the muster roll of the 82nd:

> *The colored detachment were promptly brought up in front of the Episcopal Church, behind which one company of home guards were posted. They dismounted under a galling fire of buck ball delivered at a range of thirty yards and, fixing their bayonets, charged over the church yard fence compelling the enemy's company to surrender, killing and wounding some eighteen.*

Not all of the Southerners, however, were ready to surrender. Captain George H. Maynard of the 82nd U.S.C.I. recorded that he ordered his men to stop shooting as soon as he saw signs that the Confederates were laying down their arms. "No sooner had the Union troops ceased firing than they immediately reopened fire," he wrote, "killing one of our boys, which infuriated us."

A few minutes later, Norwood's men tried to surrender again but the Federals now how difficulty controlling their own troops. Union soldiers fired a volley into the ranks of Norwood's men after they had put down their weapons, killing one and wounding several others. Maynard later received a Congressional Medal of Honor in part for what he did next:

> *I at once dismounted and rushed into the graveyard, just in time to knock away a musket placed at the head of a prisoner, and threatened to blow out the brains of the first man who dared to shoot a prisoner. This course prevented a general massacre of our captured foes, numbering 108.*

Even then, not all of the Confederates would surrender. Several men inside St. Luke's Church and two nearby homes continued to shoot at the Federals outside, refusing all demands to throw down their arms. Desperate now to bring the fighting to a close, Colonel Zulavsky ordered the buildings set afire to force these men out. A young child named Armstrong Purdee, only eight years old and the son of an enslaved laborer on the John R. Waddell plantation northwest of Marianna, had joined hundreds of other slaves following in the steps of the Union column. He witnessed the Battle of Marianna from the back of a soldier's horse and was only about 40 steps away when the orders came down to burn St. Luke's Episcopal Church:

> *All of the soldiers were off their horses. Orders were given to fire the church. Three men, two with long poles, and one with what seemed to me to be a can, threw something up on the church and the other two having something on the end of their poles, seemed to rub it as high as the poles would reach, after which something like twisted paper was lighted and placed to whatever was put on the church and it blazed up. Men were shot down as they came out of the building.*

The church was torched at its southwest corner and at least four of the men inside never made it out. The Southerners who burned to death were later identified as John C. Carter, Littleton Myrick, Francis "Frank" Allen and Woodbury "Woody" Nickels.

The nearby homes of Dr. R.A. Sanders and Mrs. Caroline Hunter were burned at the same time. The Hunter home stood directly across Lafayette Street from the church and was already in flames when it was discovered that a woman and her newborn baby were still in one of the upstairs bedrooms. Several Union soldiers ran into the burning building and saved them by wrapping them in a mattress and dropping them from a window into the arms of other soldiers who were waiting below. The rescue was documented by Confederate surgeon Henry Robinson, who heard it the next day from survivors of the battle.

According to legend, another remarkable rescue also took place that afternoon. According to the "Reminiscences" of an eyewitness to the battle, one of the Union officers objected when Colonel Zulavsky ordered the burning of the church. This officer, 20-year-old Major Nathan Cutler of the 2nd Maine Cavalry, supposedly tried to have the orders countermanded, but they were repeated and the structure soon went up in flames. According to Mrs. Daniel Love, Major Cutler was a pious and brave man. Unwilling to stand by while the church and its Bible were destroyed, he dashed through the kerosene-fueled flames and saved the St. Luke's Bible from its lectern. Shortly after he emerged from the church, however, he was confronted by two young boys from Norwood's company. They ordered him to halt and he wheeled on them with his saber, but then saw how young they were and was unable to strike. They had no such reservations and blasted him from his horse with shotgun blasts.

The story of Cutler's courage and chivalry became quite well known in Marianna within weeks of the battle. Severely injured in the engagement, he remained in a bed at the home of Mayor Thomas M. White for months, recuperating from his wounds. He was treated kindly by local citizens and remained in Marianna until he was well enough to be sent away to prison at

Macon and Andersonville. He returned after the war at the head of a detachment of Union occupation troops and, unlike most of his counterparts, was well-received by the people of the community.

It is a fascinating story, but could it be true? The most significant piece of evidence, of course, is the Bible itself. Not only did it survive the 1865 fire, but somehow was also rescued during another blaze that destroyed the replacement sanctuary during the 1940s. The edges of the Bible, in fact, show smoke damage from one of the fires.

The eyewitness was a young girl at the time of the battle but saw some of the fighting from the home of her grandparents on East Jackson Street. In her "Reminiscences" she said that she heard the story from the major's own lips. This is certainly possible. Mayor White's home, where Cutler was treated after the battle, stood at the intersection of Jackson and Madison Streets, diagonally across from the Jackson County Courthouse. The home of her grandparents was just a few doors away. Major Cutler often visited the White family when he returned to Marianna after the war and he undoubtedly came into contact with neighbors.

Mrs. Love's account is further strengthened by the fact that she was a family member of Frank Baltzell. Only thirteen years old at the time of the battle, Frank was one of the two young home guard members who confronted and shot the major.

The Cutler story also attracted the attention of John Carter, an early 20th century Marianna resident and historian. Mr. Carter became interested in the legend while trying to help the St. Luke's Parish secure Congressional reimbursement for losses sustained during the Battle of Marianna. He learned from the War Department that Major Cutler was still alive and living in Brooklyn, New York, so he traveled there to visit him:

> *...I told him of the town in general, and of the esteem in which the people still held him on account of his broadmindedness, and especially for his clemency of two young men who shot him off his horse, causing him to remain in Marianna for several weeks in a wounded bed. At this his face lightened up as if to speak of the present. He said, "Ah, yes, those dear boys." He told me how they "literally peppered" him with shot, and that he could have cut them down with his saber while they were in the act of shooting, but they were so young and so gallant it seemed a pity to cut them down, and he sat on his horse until they actually shot him off before he would maim them.*

Cutler did not, however, claim to have saved the Bible from St. Luke's Church. He related to Mr. Carter what he could remember of the incident:

Chapter Thirteen

He said that he did not remember all the circumstances, as he was shot from his horse about that time, but he afterwards learned that an express order was given to fire the church. Someone from the Federal forces protested, but the command from the same source was repeated, at which kerosene swabs were run up the sides of the building, the flames licked furiously upward and the whole church stood ablaze, and soon burned to the ground.

The major's account of the burning was strikingly similar to that written by Armstrong Purdee, down to the use of swabs to spread kerosene on the sides of the building to help spread the flames. His recollections appear to be those of someone who witnessed the scene first hand, although he certainly could have already been wounded at that point.

Another eyewitness, Surgeon George Martin of the 2nd Maine Cavalry, saw Major Cutler go down at Marianna and treated him for his wounds after the battle:

I saw Major Cutler wounded at Marianna. He was charging at the head of his command down the main street when a volley was fired by the Rebs from the churchyard, making 8 wounds in the left leg, thigh and forearm. His horse fell dead, riddled with bullets. I had him taken to the mayor's house and dressed his wounds. His arm was severely fractured, and we were obliged to leave him there when we retreated the next day. I think his ankle was also broken.

Cutler confirmed Martin's account in his own 1880 application for a government pension, reporting that he was wounded "while leading a charge through the streets of that town." He stated that he received eight wounds in the battle, breaking the femur and tibia of his left leg and thigh and fracturing the bones of his left forearm and wrist.

Based on these accounts, it appears likely that Cutler was wounded prior to the burning of the church. Considering the severity of his wounds, he probably was capable of doing little after that point. He identified Frank Baltzell as one of the youths who shot him, so that part of the story is undoubtedly true. In his interview with Mr. Carter, he also confirmed that someone in the Union force objected to the orders to burn St. Luke's and his description of how the church was fired matches almost precisely with Armstrong Purdee's account. He probably saw the burning for himself.

While these facts raise questions as to whether Cutler could have been the individual who saved the Bible, they in no way discredit the story that one of the Union officers did so. In fact, by confirming that someone in the attacking forces objected to the orders to burn the church, Cutler's account actually adds strong supporting evidence to the legend. His confirmation that he was shot by Frank Baltzell and another youth also is of value in adding support to another critical part of the story.

Curiously, long after his interview with the major, Mr. Carter wrote a history of St. Luke's in which he repeated the story as truth. This could imply that he believed the story, but felt the major was simply being modest in the interview.

The legend of the Bible of St. Luke's probably will forever remain one of the mysteries of the Battle of Marianna. Enough details of the story can be confirmed that it appears likely that the story, at least in some form, is true. Whether or not Major Nathan Cutler was the individual responsible, someone saved the Bible from St. Luke's Church. It remains there to this day, a treasured memory of a long ago event.

Figure 39: Major Nathan Cutler, 2nd Maine Cavalry

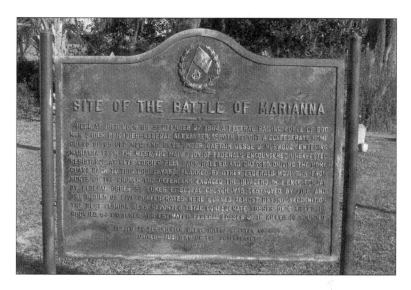

Figure 40: Battle of Marianna Marker, St. Luke's Episcopal Church

Figure 41: St. Luke's Episcopal Church, Marianna

Figure 42: Confederate Graves at Moss Hill Church, Holmes Valley

Figure 43: Bridge at Hard Labor Creek, near the site of the Battle of Vernon

Chapter Fourteen

The Battle of Vernon, Florida

One of the least known encounters of the Civil War in Florida took place as Union troops were returning to Pensacola from their September 27, 1864, attack on the city of Marianna. As they passed through Washington County, the Federals ran head on into a small company of home guards from Vernon that was trying to respond to a call for help from neighboring Jackson County. So far as is known, the skirmish was not described in any official reports of the Marianna raid. Over the years it became one of the legends of Washington County, a story about which little could be proved and yet much was told.[*]

In the hours before the Battle of Marianna, Confederate officers in the city sent out couriers to call for help from home guard companies throughout the region. A number of these units, including one at Vernon, had formed in Florida following a July 1864 executive order from Governor John Milton requiring all male citizens over the age of 16 to organize themselves into military companies to help repel expected invasions. More than 38 of these companies mustering over 3,500 men were organized in Florida. Many of these soldiers were boys much younger than the age of 16.

The home guards were not full-time soldiers. They gathered on weekends to drill and were subject to be called out during times of emergency or occasionally to perform guard or scouting duty. Otherwise they went about their normal lives.

Washington County at the time of the Civil War covered a much larger geographic area than it does today. The county stretched from Jackson and Holmes Counties on the north all the way to the Gulf of Mexico on the south and encompassed all of the areas around St. Andrews Bay that are today part of Bay County. The modern cities of Panama City, Panama City Beach and Chipley did not exist during the 1860s, although there was a small resort community at old St. Andrews on the bay. Despite its size, the county was sparsely populated. Only 2,154 people lived in this vast expanse at the time of the 1860 census and since St. Andrews had been evacuated by 1864, the population was undoubtedly even lower by the time of the Marianna raid.

---

[*] The Battle of Vernon is one of the incidents described in detail in *The Battle of Marianna, Florida,* a book by this author. For more information, please visit www.battleofmarianna.net.

Two Egg, Florida

Most of the people in the county worked on small farms and according to the 1860 census only 56 were slaveholders. A total of five churches served the entire county. One of these, Moss Hill United Methodist Church in Holmes Valley, still stands. Holmes Valley was the name given to the rich farmlands along Holmes Creek, one of the earliest settled and most productive areas in the county. Other key communities included Vernon, then the county seat, Orange Hill (then called Hickory Hill) and the Econfina settlement on Econfina Creek.

When Governor Milton ordered the formation of the state home guards, Washington County had only enough men remaining to form a single company. Everyone else of military age was either already in the service or had defected to the Federal camps around Pensacola. The sheriff of the county, Abram Skipper, was among the defectors.

As required by the instructions of the state adjutant general, the Washington County company mustered at Vernon, the county seat. The men elected W.B. Jones as their captain. A former Vernon justice of the peace, Jones had served as a second lieutenant with Company K of the 6th Florida Infantry earlier in the war. He became sick and disabled while serving in Tennessee and was released from service and allowed to return home. There is some evidence that he may have formed a volunteer company prior to the governor's order, but if so then this unit was merged into the state home guards when they were organized in 1864.

A muster roll of Jones' company has not survived, so it is impossible to know exactly how many members his unit mustered. Estimates in witness statements accompanying state pension applications vary, but the minimum number was probably no less than 30.

On the morning of September 27, 1864, as Union troops were advancing on Marianna, officers there sent out riders to call in home guard units from throughout the area to help defend the city. The call went out too late, however, and most of the unit commanders did not learn of the emergency until well after the Battle of Marianna was over. This was the case with Captain Jones and his men.

Considering the distance, it probably took the better part of the day for a courier to reach Vernon. Even once he knew of the call for help, it took time for Captain Jones to assemble his men. In later years when survivors of the company filed applications for state pensions, most indicated that they assembled at Vernon on the morning of September 28th. This is reasonable as it probably would have taken that long for Jones to alert his men and get them together.

In addition to the regular members of his company, the captain forced every available man into service, regardless of age. Several men well over the age of 60 later recorded that they were conscripted into the service on the morning of the 28th. How much Captain Jones was able to increase the strength of his unit through such measures is not clear, but the company probably included at least 50 men when it rode out from Vernon later that morning.

Chapter Fourteen

A direct road then connected Vernon with Marianna. Chipley had not yet been founded, so this route led northeast to Orange (Hickory) Hill and from there on to Marianna where it entered the city along the route of today's Orange Avenue. Although neither side knew it, the Federal force that had attacked Marianna was riding west on the same road. The stage was set for a tragic confrontation.

Having captured Marianna on the afternoon of the 27th, suffering heavy casualties in the process, the Federal column left the city during the predawn hours of September 28th via the road to Orange Hill and Vernon. Brigadier General Alexander Asboth, who commanded the raid, had been severely wounded in the Battle of Marianna and was now being carried on a bed placed in the back of a wagon. Command of the column had fallen to Colonel L.L. Zulavsky of the 82nd U.S. Colored Infantry, a no nonsense officer who had brought the fight in Marianna to a close by burning a church and two nearby homes.

In addition to its 700 mounted soldiers, the Union column left Marianna with a herd of 200 horses and mules, 400 head of cattle and 17 wagons loaded with captured arms and supplies. Over 600 liberated slaves followed in the wake of the column, determined to walk to freedom.

The soldiers reached Orange Hill and, according to legend, halted on the grounds of the old Baptist academy there for their noon meal. The academy stood on the grounds of today's Orange Hill United Methodist Church, adjacent to the large plantation of David Porter Everett. From there the troops headed down the hill and continued on in the direction of Vernon.

That afternoon, the Union soldiers came down the hill to the crossing at Hard Labor Creek near today's Washington Church and Cemetery, much more concerned about Confederate cavalry that was rumored to be pursuing them than any force that might be ahead. Captain Jones and his men approached the crossing from the opposite direction at precisely the same time. John J. Wright, a member of Jones' company, recalled what happened next in his pension application:

> *...We suddenly met the Northern soldiers and they demanded that we surrender, fighting opened and a large man by the name of Pierce was killed near me. I was wounded, and was taken home. Captain Jones was captured, and was taken away.*

The exact sequence of events that led to the opening of the battle is obscured in mystery. Legend holds that a member of Jones' company named Stephen Pierce, the "large man by the name of Pierce" mentioned in Wright's account, verbally taunted or cursed the enemy soldiers when they made their demand that Jones and his men surrender. They responded by opening fire on the Confederates, scattering them with a single volley. Pierce was supposedly dragged away behind a gallberry bush and executed, although Wright's account suggests that he was actually killed in the brief firefight.

At the time of the Battle of Vernon, Stephen Pierce was a 46-year-old farmer who supported his wife, Jane, and at least six children. He owned no slaves and his total worth at the time of the 1860 census was only $100. Although he is often identified as a member of the 4th Florida Infantry who was home on leave, he actually was no longer a member of the regiment. Like many of his neighbors Pierce had enlisted in the "Washington County Invincibles" in September of 1861. The unit became Company H of the 4th Florida Infantry and Pierce served with it in the Army of Tennessee, fighting at Shiloh and Stones River. He received a medical discharge in 1863, however, and returned home to his farm. He joined Captain Jones' company in August of 1864 after Governor Milton ordered the formation of the state home guards.

So far as is known, Pierce was the only man killed in the Battle of Vernon. John J. Wright, mentioned above, was the only man known to have been wounded. In his pension application, he reported that he was shot twice in the skirmish. "I have lost the use of my right arm," he wrote, "never could use it as good after I was shot in the shoulder. I was also hit in the left leg that soon got well and has not bothered me but little."

Another member of Jones' company, M.L. Lassiter, wrote years later that he was chased from the scene at Hard Labor Creek in a running skirmish that continued all the way to Vernon:

> ...On our way to Marianna we met a company of Federals, near Hard Labor Creek, and Jones company was captured and taken to Ship Island Prison. I made my escape on horseback and outran them. I was pursued all the way back to Vernon and shot at many times but escaped without injury.

In either the initial melee or the running fight that followed, Captain Jones and ten of his men were captured. Four of these men, Andrew and James Gable of the 6th Florida Infantry and H.R. and B.A. Walker of the 1st Florida Reorganized Infantry, were Confederate regulars home on leave who volunteered to fight with the home guards. Also captured were Enoch Johns, Shadrick Johns, John Nelson, Cary Taylor, Freeman Irwin and Nathaniel Miller. Irwin had represented Washington County at Florida's secession convention in 1861 and Taylor was a former Washington County sheriff.

The Federals pursued the remnants of Jones' company on into Vernon, but the rest of the Confederates managed to escape. The raiders halted in the town to rest for a few hours, but moved on later in the night and continued their march to Point Washington on Choctawhatchee Bay. Before they left, however, they released several of the younger prisoners they had taken in Marianna. One of these, 13-year-old Frank Baltzell, told his family that he had fallen asleep under a bench and when he woke up, the Federals were gone. The Union troops reached Point Washington without further incident.

The body of Stephen Pierce was taken up the hill from Hard Labor Creek and buried at what became Hard Labor or Washington Cemetery. According to tradition his was the first grave there, but a nearby headstone displays an older date.

The families of the men captured in the Battle of Vernon were left to fend for themselves. Sixty-three year old Enoch Johns, for example, left behind his wife and four children. The youngest of his children, also named Enoch, was only four years old when he watched his father mount a horse and ride away to fight. He never saw or heard from him again. By the end of the war, Mrs. Johns was desperate and decided to leave Washington County and seek help from her family in Alabama. She hired a wagon to transport the family's goods, but the wagon and its driver disappeared along the way and she and her children reached their relatives in total destitution. Tragically, her family members were on the verge of starvation themselves and they turned the unfortunate woman and her children away.

She slowly made her way back to Washington County where the little family built a hut of tree branches in the woods. Although they too were suffering, neighbors took pity on them and procured a job for her at a local grist mill. Since they had no cash themselves, the owners paid her daily wages in corn meal so that she could feed the children. Enoch later remembered a pathetic scene that took place one afternoon when his mother came home from work with her day's wages of corn mill secured in her apron. One of the young children was excited to see her and ran out to greet her. In the resulting collision, the precious corn meal was spilled into the dirt and the family went hungry that night.

The stories of the prisoners themselves were equally tragic. Carried away by the Union troops, they were shipped to prison camps first at New Orleans and then Ship Island, Mississippi, before finally reaching the disease-ridden compound at Elmira, New York. Cary Taylor and Enoch Johns died there of small pox on December 27, 1864, less than two months after the Battle of Vernon. Shadrick Johns and Cary Taylor tried to secure their freedom by offering to swear oaths of allegiance to the United States government. They both said they had been "conscripted, ordered out by the Governor to resist a raiding party, and had been captured the same day." Although they were seriously ill and over 50 years old, their request was denied and both men remained at Elmira until the end of the war.

Three more of the Washington County prisoners died at the prison. Andrew Gable lost his life to pneumonia on January 1, 1865. Freeman Irwin died from illness on February 7th and Nathaniel Miller followed on March 13th. Captain Jones, according to his wife, returned from prison greatly enfeebled from sickness, but survived another thirty years.

Markers for some of these men can be found today at the cemetery next to Moss Hill Methodist Church near Vernon, where they once attended services. A wooden bridge crosses Hard Labor Creek near the site of Vernon battle and the traces of the old road can still be seen nearby. Washington Church, a beautiful rustic structure, stands nearby at the top of hill. The grave of Stephen Pierce can be found in the cemetery across the road. The men who died at Elmira were buried there, far away from their homes, neighbors and families. Enoch Johns, who was last seen riding away on his horse, rests there to this day.

No markers or monuments recount the history of the Battle of Vernon, yet for the people involved it was a significant event nonetheless. Long relegated to the status of legend, the skirmish demonstrates through the mists of time how desperate things had become during the final days of the War Between the States. The tragic stories of the Vernon captives and their families are but a few of the hundreds of thousands of similar stories that can still be told about a war that most Americans no longer even remember.

Washington County has changed greatly since the days of the Civil War. The southern half of the county was carved off to create modern Bay County, where Panama City Beach and the surrounding area is now the playground of a nation. The county seat has moved as well. A new community named Chipley grew in the northern part of the county after the railroad came through in the years after the war. Despite such changes, however, the county remains a picturesque and beautiful place, blessed with charming and friendly people.

Figure 44: Grave of Stephen Pierce, Victim of the Battle of Vernon

Figure 45: Historic Moss Hill Church, Washington County

Figure 46: Washington Church, near the scene of the Battle of Vernon

Figure 47: Two Egg, Florida

Figure 48: The Garden of Eden, Liberty County

About the Author

A native of the Two Egg area, Dale Cox grew up immersed in the history and folklore of Northwest Florida, Southwest Georgia and Southeast Alabama. A descendent of the noted American pioneer Daniel Boone, he lists among his ancestors many early settlers of both Jackson and Washington Counties, Florida, and Decatur County, Georgia. He is also descended from the noted Native American leader Efau Emathla (William Brown), a chief of the Euchee branch of the Creek Nation.

His unique cultural heritage played a critical role in the formation of his life-long love of history and passion for preservation. He began studying and writing about local history at an early age, producing a series of articles for his hometown newspaper, *The Jackson County Floridan*, at the age of twelve.

In addition to studies in archaeology and anthropology, Cox has written or contributed to five books on Northwest Florida, including the present volume. Among these is his 2007 book, *The Battle of Marianna, Florida*. Critically acclaimed as a groundbreaking study in Northwest Florida history, the book was his first national release. A companion volume on the Battle of Natural Bridge, Florida, is also now available in national release.

He served as an editor of noted Florida historian E.W. Carswell's monumental, *Washington – Florida's Twelfth County* and has penned numerous newspaper, magazine and internet articles on topics of historical interest. Other works include *The History of Jackson County, Florida: The Early Years*; *The Early History of Gadsden County*; *The Battle of Natural Bridge, Florida;* and, *The Battle of Massard Prairie*.

Noted for his abilities as a journalist and manager, Cox has worked for a number of America's largest media companies. Most recently he managed two newsrooms for the broadcast division of The New York Times Company. The son of Clinton and Pearl Cox of Jackson County, Florida, he is the father of two grown sons, William and Alan Cox. He lives in the piney woods of Northwest Florida.

Two Egg, Florida

Figure 49: Two Egg, Florida

Figure 50: The Apalachicola River

Other Books by Dale Cox

The Battle of Marianna, Florida

A detailed account of the Battle of Marianna, one of Florida's
least known yet most significant Civil War encounters.

$19.95

The Battle of Natural Bridge, Florida

A history of the Civil War battle that preserved Tallahassee's
status as the only Southern capital east of the Mississippi
not captured by Union forces.

$19.95

The History of Jackson County, Florida: The Early Years

A detailed history of the exploration, settlement and development of Florida's
third county, this volume explores Spanish missions, Indian villages, Seminole
War battlefields, ghost towns, Florida's lost county and more.

$24.95

The Early History of Gadsden County
A well-researched and thoroughly readable history of Gadsden County, Florida,
this book explores this fascinating county from the days of its earliest exploration
through the brutal era of the Civil War.

$24.95

Two Egg, Florida

8227658R0

Made in the USA
Lexington, KY
16 January 2011